FREMDSPRACHENTEXTE

John Irving

# The Pension Grillparzer

Herausgegeben von
Hans-Joachim Lehnig



Philipp Reclam jun. Stuttgart

Diese Ausgabe darf nur in der Bundesrepublik Deutschland, in Österreich und in der Schweiz vertrieben werden.

RECLAMS UNIVERSAL-BIBLIOTHEK Nr. 19758

Gesamtherstellung: Reclam, Ditzingen. Printed in Germany 2009
RECLAM, UNIVERSAL-BIBLIOTHEK und RECLAMS UNIVERSAL-BIBLIOTHEK sind eingetragene Marken der Philipp Reclam jun. GmbH & Co., Stuttgart
ISBN 978-3-15-019758-5

www.reclam.de

My father worked for the Austrian Tourist Bureau. It was my mother's idea that our family travel with him when he went on the road as a Tourist Bureau spy. My mother and brother and I would accompany him on his secretive missions to uncover the discourtesy, the dust, the badly cooked food, the shortcuts taken by Austria's restaurants and hotels and pensions. We were instructed to create difficulties whenever we could, never to order exactly what was on the menu, to imitate a foreigner's odd requests – the hours we would like to have our baths, the need for aspirin and directions to the zoo. We were instructed to be civilized but troublesome; and when the visit was over, we reported to my father in the car.

My mother would say, "The hairdresser is always

[Titel] **Grillparzer:** Franz G. (1791–1872), österreichischer Dramatiker.
4 **spy:** Spion; hier: Kundschafter.
5 **secretive:** geheim, heimlich.
**mission:** Auftrag.
5f. **discourtesy:** Unhöflichkeit.
7 **shortcut:** Einsparung, Sparmaßnahme.
10 **menu:** Speisekarte.
**odd:** sonderbar, ausgefallen.
11 **request:** Bitte, Wunsch.
13f. **troublesome:** lästig, störend.

closed in the morning. But they make suitable recommendations outside. I guess it's all right, provided they don't claim to have a hairdresser actually *in* the hotel."

"Well, they *do* claim it," my father would say. He'd note this in a giant pad.

I was always the driver. I said, "The car is parked off the street, but someone put fourteen kilometers on the gauge between the time we handed it over to the doorman and picked it up at the hotel garage."

"That is a matter to report directly to the management," my father said, jotting it down.

"The toilet leaked," I said.

"I couldn't open the door to the W.C.," said my brother, Robo.

"Robo," Mother said, "you always have trouble with doors."

"Was that supposed to be Class C?" I asked.

"I'm afraid not," Father said. "It is still listed as Class B." We drove for a short while in silence; our most serious judgment concerned changing a ho-

1 **suitable:** geeignet.
1f. **recommendation:** Empfehlung.
2f. **provided:** unter der Voraussetzung, sofern.
6 **giant:** riesig, groß.
**pad:** Schreibblock.
7f. **to park off the street:** im Parkhaus unterstellen.
9 **gauge:** Kilometeranzeige, Kilometerstand.
13 **to jot s.th. down:** etwas notieren, aufschreiben.
14 **to leak:** undicht sein.

tel's or a pension's rating. We did not suggest reclassification frivolously.

"I think this calls for a letter to the management," Mother suggested. "Not too nice a letter, but not a really rough one. Just state the facts."

"Yes, I rather liked him," Father said. He always made a point of getting to meet the managers.

"Don't forget the business of them driving our car," I said. "That's really unforgivable."

"And the eggs were bad," said Robo; he was not yet ten and his judgments were not considered seriously.

We became a far harsher team of evaluators when my grandfather died and we inherited grandmother – my mother's mother, who thereafter accompanied us on our travels. A regal dame, Johanna was accustomed to Class A travel, and my father's duties more frequently called for investigations of Class B and Class C lodgings. They were the places, the B and C hotels (and the pensions), that most interested the tourists. At restaurants we

1 **rating:** Bewertung, Einstufung (in Qualitätskategorien).
1 f. **reclassification:** Neueinstufung.
2 **frivolously:** leichtfertig.
5 **rough:** barsch, grob.
13 **harsh:** scharf, streng.
**evaluator:** Bewerter.
14 **to inherit:** erben.
15 **thereafter:** danach, von da an.
16 **regal:** königlich (auftretend).
18 f. **investigation:** Überprüfung, Nachforschung.

did a little better. People who couldn't afford the classy places to sleep were still interested in the best places to eat.

"I shall not have dubious food tested on me," Johanna told us. "This strange employment may give you all glee about having free vacations, but I can see there is a terrible price paid: the anxiety of not knowing what sort of quarters you'll have for the night. Americans may find it charming that we still have rooms without private baths and toilets, but I am an old woman and I'm not charmed by walking down a public corridor in search of cleanliness and my relievement. Anxiety is only half of it. Actual diseases are possible – and not only from food. If the bed is questionable, I promise I shan't put my head down. And the children are young and impressionable; you should think of the clientele in some of these lodgings and seriously ask yourselves about the influences." My mother and father nodded; they said nothing. "Slow down!" Grandmother said sharply to me. "You're just a young boy

4 **dubious:** fragwürdig.
5 f. **to give s.o. glee:** jdn. in beste Stimmung versetzen.
7 **anxiety:** Sorge.
8 **quarters** (pl.): Quartier, Unterkunft.
12 f. **in search … relievement** (idiom.): auf der Suche nach Bad und Toilette (*relievement:* Erleichterung).
16 f. **impressionable:** für Eindrücke empfänglich.
17 **clientele:** Kundenkreis, Publikum.
19 f. **to nod:** nicken.

who likes to show off." I slowed down. "Vienna," Grandmother sighed. "In Vienna I always stayed at the Ambassador."

"Johanna, the Ambassador is not under investigation," Father said.

"I should think not," Johanna said. "I suppose we're not even headed toward a Class A place?"

"Well, it's a B trip," my father admitted. "For the most part."

"I trust," Grandmother said, "that you mean there is one A place en route?"

"No," Father admitted. "There is one C place."

"It's okay," Robo said. "There are fights in Class C."

"I should imagine so," Johanna said.

"It's a Class C pension, very small," Father said, as if the size of the place forgave it.

"And they're applying for a B," said Mother.

"But there have been some complaints," I added.

"I'm sure there have," Johanna said.

"And animals," I added. My mother gave me a look.

"Animals?" said Johanna.

"Animals," I admitted.

1 **to show off:** angeben, eine Schau abziehen.
7 **to be headed toward s.th.:** etwas ansteuern.
10 **to trust:** erwarten.
11 **en route:** auf dem Weg.
19 **complaint:** Beschwerde.

"A *suspicion* of animals," my mother corrected me.

"Yes, be fair," Father said.

"Oh, wonderful!" Grandmother said. "A suspicion of animals. Their hair on the rugs? Their terrible waste in the corners! Did you know that my asthma reacts, severely, to any room in which there has recently been a cat?"

"The complaint was not about cats," I said. My mother elbowed me sharply.

"Dogs?" Johanna said. "Rabid dogs! Biting you on the way to the bathroom."

"No," I said. "Not dogs."

"Bears!" Robo cried.

But my mother said, "We don't know for sure about the bear, Robo."

"This isn't serious," Johanna said.

"Of course it's not serious!" Father said. "How could there be bears in a pension?"

"There was a letter saying so," I said. "Of course, the Tourist Bureau assumed it was a crank complaint. But then there was another sighting – and a second letter claiming there had been a bear."

1 **a suspicion of s.th.:** ein Verdacht auf etwas.
5 **rug:** (kleiner) Teppich, Brücke.
6 **waste:** Exkrement, Ausscheidung.
11 **rabid:** tollwütig.
21 **crank:** verschroben.
22 **there was another sighting** (idiom.): es gab die gleiche Beobachtung.

My father used the rear-view mirror to scowl at me, but I thought that if we were all supposed to be in on the investigation, it would be wise to have Grandmother on her toes.

"It's probably not a real bear," Robo said, with obvious disappointment.

"A man in a bear suit!" Johanna cried. "What unheard-of perversion is *that?* A *beast* of a man sneaking about in disguise! Up to what? It's a man in a bear suit, I know it is," she said. "I want to go to that one *first!* If there's going to be a Class C experience on this trip, let's get it over with as soon as possible."

"But we haven't got reservations for tonight," Mother said.

"Yes, we might as well give them a chance to be at their best," Father said. Although he never revealed to his victims that he worked for the Tourist Bureau, Father believed that reservations were simply a decent way of allowing the personnel to be as prepared as they could be.

1 **rear-view mirror:** Rückspiegel.
1 f. **to scowl at s.o.:** jdn. finster anblicken.
3 f. **to have s.o. on his/her toes** (idiom.): jdn. (auf etwas) einstellen, vorbereiten, vorwarnen.
9 **to sneak about:** herumschleichen.
**in disguise:** verkleidet.
12 **to get s.th. over with:** etwas hinter sich bringen.
17 f. **to reveal:** verraten, enthüllen.
20 **decent:** anständig.
**personnel:** Personal.

"I'm sure we don't need to make a reservation in a place frequented by men who disguise themselves as animals," Johanna said. "I'm sure there is *always* a vacancy there. I'm sure the guests are regularly dying in their beds – of fright, or else of whatever unspeakable injury the madman in the foul bear suit does to them."

"It's probably a *real* bear," Robo said, hopefully – for in the turn the conversation was taking, Robo certainly saw that a real bear would be preferable to Grandmother's imagined ghoul. Robo had no fear, I think, of a real bear.

I drove us as inconspicuously as possible to the dark, dwarfed corner of Planken and Seilergasse. We were looking for the Class C pension that wanted to be a B.

"No place to park," I said to Father, who was already making note of that in his pad.

I double-parked and we sat in the car and peered

2 **to frequent:** aufsuchen, häufig besuchen.
4 **vacancy:** freies Zimmer.
5 **fright:** Schreck.
6 **injury:** Verletzung.
7 **foul:** widerlich, abscheulich.
10 f. **to be preferable to s.th.:** besser als etwas sein.
11 **ghoul:** Unhold.
13 **inconspicuously:** unauffällig.
14 **dwarfed:** unscheinbar.
**Planken/Seilergasse:** Plankengasse, Seilergasse; konkrete Wiener Straßennamen (s. Abb. S. 85).
19 **to double-park:** in zweiter Reihe parken.
**to peer:** spähen, schauen.

up at the Pension Grillparzer; it rose only four slender stories between a pastry shop and a Tabak Trafik.

"See?" Father said. "No bears."

"No *men*, I hope," said Grandmother.

"They come at night," Robo said, looking cautiously up and down the street.

We went inside to meet the manager, a Herr Theobald, who instantly put Johanna on her guard.

"Three generations traveling together!" he cried. "Like the old days," he added, especially to Grandmother, "before all these divorces and the young people wanting apartments by themselves. This is a *family* pension! I just wish you had made a reservation – so I could put you more closely together."

"We're not accustomed to sleeping in the same room," Grandmother told him.

"Of course not!" Theobald cried. "I just meant that I wished your *rooms* could be closer together." This worried Grandmother, clearly.

2 **slender:** schmal, eng.
**story:** Stockwerk, Etage (BE *storey*).
**pastry shop:** Konditorei.

2f. **Tabak Trafik:** in Österreich übliche Bezeichnung für einen Tabakladen.

6f. **cautiously:** vorsichtig.

9 **to put s.o. on his/her guard:** jdn. auf der Hut sein lassen, misstrauisch machen.

12 **divorce:** (Ehe-)Scheidung.

16 **to be accustomed to doing s.th.:** daran gewöhnt sein, etwas zu tun, üblicherweise etwas tun.

"How far apart must we be put?" she asked.

"Well, I've only two rooms left," he said. "And only one of them is large enough for the two boys to share with their parents."

"And my room is how far from theirs?" Johanna asked coolly.

"You're right across from the W.C.!" Theobald told her, as if this were a plus.

But as we were shown to our rooms, Grandmother staying with Father – contemptuously to the rear of our procession – I heard her mutter, "This is not how I conceived of my retirement. Across the hall from a W.C., listening to all the visitors."

"Not one of these rooms is the same," Theobald told us. "The furniture is all from my family." We could believe it. The one large room Robo and I were to share with my parents was a half-sized museum of knickknacks, every dresser with a different style of knob. On the other hand, the sink had

8 **plus:** Pluspunkt.
10 **contemptuously:** voller Verachtung.
11 **to the rear of s.th.:** hinter etwas, am Ende von etwas.
**to mutter:** murmeln.
12 **to conceive of s.th.:** sich etwas vorstellen.
**retirement:** Ruhestand.
18f. **a half-sized museum** (coll.): ein mittleres Museum.
19 **knickknack** (coll.): Schnickschnack.
**dresser:** Kommode.
20 **knob:** Griff, Knauf; hier: Beschlag.

brass faucets and the headboard of the bed was carved. I could see my father balancing things up for future notation in the giant pad.

"You may do that later," Johanna informed him. "Where do *I* stay?"

As a family, we dutifully followed Theobald and my grandmother down the long, twining hall, my father counting the paces to the W.C. The hall rug was thin, the color of a shadow. Along the walls were old photographs of speed-skating teams – on their feet the strange blades curled up at the tips like court jesters' shoes or the runners of ancient sleds.

Robo, running far ahead, announced his discovery of the W.C.

Grandmother's room was full of china, polished wood, and the hint of mold. The drapes were

1 **brass faucet:** Wasserhahn aus Messing.
**headboard:** Kopfteil (eines Bettgestells).
2 **to be carved:** mit Schnitzereien verziert sein.
**to balance s.th. up:** etwas gegeneinander abwägen.
7 **twining:** gewunden (*to twine:* sich winden).
9 **the color of a shadow:** etwa: verblichen.
10 **speed-skating:** Eisschnelllauf.
11 **blade:** Gleitschiene.
**tip:** Spitze.
12 **court jester:** Hofnarr.
**runner:** (Schlitten-)Kufe.
13 **sled:** Schlitten.
17 **hint:** Anflug, Spur.
**mold:** Moder, Schimmel.
**drapes** (pl.): Vorhang.

damp. The bed had an unsettling ridge at its center, like fur risen on a dog's spine – it was almost as if a very slender body lay stretched beneath the bedspread.

Grandmother said nothing, and when Theobald reeled out of the room like a wounded man who's been told he'll live, Grandmother asked my father, "On what basis can the Pension Grillparzer hope to get a B?"

"Quite decidedly C," Father said.

"Born C and will die C," I said.

"I would say, myself," Grandmother told us, "that it was E or F."

In the dim tearoom a man without a tie sang a Hungarian song. "It does not mean he's Hungarian," Father reassured Johanna, but she was skeptical.

"I'd say the odds are not in his favor," she suggested. She would not have tea or coffee. Robo ate a little cake, which he claimed to like. My mother

1 **unsettling:** beunruhigend.
**ridge:** Wulst.
2 **fur:** Fell.
**spine:** Wirbelsäule.
3 **slender:** schmächtig, schlank.
3f. **bedspread:** Tagesdecke.
6 **to reel:** schwanken, taumeln.
14 **dim:** dämmrig, dunkel (Zimmer).
16 **to reassure:** versichern, beruhigen.
17 **the odds are not in his favor:** es spricht (eher) nichts für ihn.

and I smoked a cigarette; she was trying to quit and I was trying to start. Therefore, we shared a cigarette between us – in fact, we'd promised never to smoke a whole one alone.

"He's a great guest," Herr Theobald whispered to my father; he indicated the singer. "He knows songs from all over."

"From Hungary, at least," Grandmother said, but she smiled.

A small man, clean-shaven but with that permanent gun-blue shadow of a beard on his lean face, spoke to my grandmother. He wore a clean white shirt (but yellow from age and laundering), suit pants, and an unmatching jacket.

"Pardon me?" said Grandmother.

"I said that I tell dreams," the man informed her.

"You *tell* dreams," Grandmother said. "Meaning, you *have* them?"

"Have them and tell them," he said mysteriously. The singer stopped singing.

"Any dream you want to know," said the singer. "He can tell it."

"I'm quite sure I don't want to know any,"

1 **to quit:** (mit etwas) aufhören.
7 **from all over** (coll.): aus der ganzen Welt.
11 **gun-blue:** grau-blau.
**lean:** hager.
13 **laundering:** Waschen.
14 **unmatching:** nicht (dazu) passend.
19 **mysteriously:** geheimnisvoll.

Grandmother said. She viewed with displeasure the ascot of dark hair bursting out at the open throat of the singer's shirt. She would not regard the man who "told" dreams at all.

"I can see you are a lady," the dream man told Grandmother. "You don't respond to just every dream that comes along."

"Certainly not," said Grandmother. She shot my father one of her how-could-you-have-let-this-happen-to-me? looks.

"But I know one," said the dream man; he shut his eyes. The singer slipped a chair forward and we suddenly realized he was sitting very close to us. Robo, though he was much too old for it, sat in Father's lap. "In a great castle," the dream man began, "a woman lay beside her husband. She was wide awake, suddenly, in the middle of the night. She woke up without the slightest idea of what had awakened her, and she felt as alert as if she'd been up for hours. It was also clear to her, without a look, a word, or a touch, that her husband was wide awake too – and just as suddenly."

1 **displeasure:** Missfallen.
2 **ascot:** zu einem Knoten gebundenes, eng anliegendes Halstuch; hier etwa: Bausch.
**to burst out:** hier: hervorquellen.
6 **to respond to s.th.:** auf etwas reagieren.
12 **to slip forward:** vorwärts schieben.
15 **lap:** Schoß.
18 **slight:** gering.
19 **alert:** (hell)wach.

"I hope this is suitable for the child to hear, ha ha," Herr Theobald said, but no one even looked at him. My grandmother folded her hands in her lap and stared at them – her knees together, her heels tucked under her straight-backed chair. My mother held my father's hand.

I sat next to the dream man, whose jacket smelled like a zoo. He said, "The woman and her husband lay awake listening for sounds in the castle, which they were only renting and did not know intimately. They listened for sounds in the courtyard, which they never bothered to lock. The village people always took walks by the castle; the village children were allowed to swing on the great courtyard door. What had woken them?"

"Bears?" said Robo, but Father touched his fingertips to Robo's mouth.

"They heard horses," said the dream man. Old Johanna, her eyes shut, her head inclined toward her lap, seemed to shudder in her stiff chair. "They heard the breathing and stamping of horses who were trying to keep still," the dream man said. "The husband reached out and touched his wife.

1 **suitable:** geeignet.
5 **to tuck:** stecken, klemmen.
**straight-backed chair:** Stuhl mit gerader, nicht gepolsteter Rückenlehne.
11 **intimately:** genau.
11 f. **courtyard:** Hof.
12 **to bother to do s.th.:** sich die Mühe machen, etwas zu tun.
20 **to shudder:** schaudern, zittern.

'Horses?' he said. The woman got out of bed and went to the courtyard window. She would swear to this day that the courtyard was full of soldiers on horseback – but *what* soldiers they were! They wore *armor!* The visors on their helmets were closed and their murmuring voices were as tinny and difficult to hear as voices on a fading radio station. Their armor clanked as their horses shifted restlessly under them.

"There was an old dry bowl of a former fountain, there in the castle's courtyard, but the woman saw that the fountain was flowing; the water lapped over the worn curb and the horses were drinking it. The knights were wary, they would not dismount; they looked up at the castle's dark windows, as if they knew they were uninvited at this watering trough – this rest station on their way, somewhere.

In the moonlight the woman saw their big shields

5 **armor:** Rüstung, Panzer.
**visor:** Visier.
6 **tinny:** blechern.
8 **to clank:** scheppern, rasseln.
**to shift:** sich hin und her bewegen.
10 **bowl:** Becken.
**former:** früher, ehemalig.
13 **to lap:** plätschern, schwappen.
**curb:** hier: Einfassung.
14 **wary:** wachsam, vorsichtig.
15 **to dismount:** absitzen, aus dem Sattel steigen.
17 **trough:** Trog.

glint. She crept back to bed and lay rigidly against her husband.

'What is it?' he asked her.

'Horses,' she told him.

'I thought so,' he said. 'They'll eat the flowers.'

'Who built this castle?' she asked him. It was a very old castle, they both knew that.

'Charlemagne,' he told her; he was going back to sleep.

But the woman lay awake, listening to the water which now seemed to be running all through the castle, gurgling in every drain, as if the old fountain were drawing water from every available source. And there were the distorted voices of the whispering knights – *Charlemagne's* soldiers speaking their dead language! To this woman, the soldiers' voices were as morbid as the eighth century and the people called Franks. The horses kept drinking.

1 **to glint:** glitzern.
**rigidly:** starr, erstarrt.
8 **Charlemagne:** Karl der Große (742–814), König der Franken und erster Kaiser des Heiligen Römischen Reiches von 800 bis 814.
12 **to gurgle:** gluckern, gurgeln.
**drain:** (Abfluss-)Rohr.
13 **available:** verfügbar.
14 **distorted:** verzerrt.
17 **morbid:** grausig, schauerlich.
18 **Franks:** Sammelbegriff für die Bevölkerung Westeuropas ab dem 9. Jh., vorher vor allem für die Bevölkerung Frankreichs und entlang des Niederrheins.

The woman lay awake a long time, waiting for the soldiers to leave; she had no fear of actual attack from them – she was sure they were on a journey and had only stopped to rest at a place they once knew. But for as long as the water ran she felt that she mustn't disturb the castle's stillness or its darkness. When she fell asleep, she thought Charlemagne's men were still there.

In the morning her husband asked her, 'Did you hear water running, too?' Yes, she had, of course. But the fountain was dry, of course, and out the window they could see that the flowers weren't eaten – and everyone knows horses eat flowers.

'Look,' said her husband; he went into the courtyard with her. 'There are *no* hoofprints, there are no droppings. We must have *dreamed* we heard horses.' She did not tell him that there were soldiers, too; or that, in her opinion, it was unlikely that two people would dream the same dream. She did not remind him that he was a heavy smoker who never smelled the soup simmering; the aroma of horses in the fresh air was too subtle for him.

She saw the soldiers, or dreamed them, twice more while they stayed there, but her husband never again woke up with her. It was always sudden.

15 **hoofprint:** Hufabdruck.
16 **droppings:** Tierexkremente; hier: ‚Pferdeäpfel'.
18 **unlikely:** unwahrscheinlich.
21 **to simmer:** sieden, brodeln.
22 **subtle:** fein.

Once she woke with the taste of metal on her tongue as if she'd touched some old, sour iron to her mouth – a sword, a chest plate, chain mail, a thigh guard. They were out there again, in colder weather. From the water in the fountain a dense fog shrouded them; the horses were snowy with frost. And there were not so many of them the next time – as if the winter or their skirmishes were reducing their numbers. The last time the horses looked gaunt to her, and the men looked more like unoccupied suits of armor balanced delicately in the saddles. The horses wore long masks of ice on their muzzles. Their breathing (or the men's breathing) was congested.

Her husband," said the dream man, "would die of a respiratory infection. But the woman did not know it when she dreamed this dream."

My grandmother looked up from her lap and slapped the dream man's beard-gray face. Robo

3 **chest plate:** Brustschild.
**chain mail:** Kettenpanzer.
4 **thigh guard:** Beinschutz (*thigh:* Oberschenkel).
6 **to shroud:** (in ein Leichentuch) einhüllen, verhüllen.
8 **skirmish:** Gefecht, (Kampf-)Geplänkel.
10 **gaunt:** ausgemergelt.
11 **unoccupied:** unbesetzt; hier: leer.
**suit of armor:** Rüstung.
13 **muzzle:** Maul (Pferd).
14 **to be congested:** blockiert sein; hier: langsam, mühsam gehen (Atem), schwerfallen.
16 **respiratory infection:** Infektion der Atemwege.
19 **to slap s.o.'s face:** jdn. ohrfeigen.

stiffened in my father's lap; my mother caught her mother's hand. The singer shoved back his chair and jumped to his feet, frightened, or ready to fight someone, but the dream man simply bowed to Grandmother and left the gloomy tearoom. It was as if he'd made a contact with Johanna that was vital but gave neither of them any joy. My father wrote something in the giant pad.

"Well, wasn't *that* some story?" said Herr Theobald. "Ha ha." He rumpled Robo's hair – something Robo always hated.

"Herr Theobald," my mother said, still holding Johanna's hand, "*my father died of a respiratory infection.*"

"Oh, dear shit," said Herr Theobald. "I'm sorry, *meine Frau*," he told Grandmother, but old Johanna would not speak to him.

We took Grandmother out to eat in a Class A restaurant, but she hardly touched her food. "That person was a gypsy," she told us. "A satanic being, and a Hungarian."

"Please, Mother," my mother said. "He couldn't have known about Father."

"He knew more than you know," Grandmother snapped.

2 **to shove back:** zurückstoßen.
5 **gloomy:** düster.
10 **to rumple:** (Haar) zerzausen.
20 **gypsy** (pej., coll.): Zigeuner(in).
25 **to snap:** fauchen, (jdn.) anfahren, (barsch) zurechtweisen.

"The schnitzel is excellent," Father said, writing in the pad. "The Gumpoldskirchner is just right with it."

"The Kalbsnieren are fine," I said.

"The eggs are okay," said Robo.

Grandmother said nothing until we returned to the Pension Grillparzer, where we noticed that the door to the W.C. was hung a foot or more off the floor, so that it resembled the bottom half of an American toilet-stall door or a saloon door in the Western movies. "I'm certainly glad I used the W.C. at the restaurant," Grandmother said. "How revolting! I shall try to pass the night without exposing myself where every passerby can peer at my ankles!"

In our family room Father said, "Didn't Johanna live in a castle? Once upon a time, I thought she and Grandpa rented some castle."

"Yes, it was before I was born," Mother said. "They rented Schloss Katzelsdorf. I saw the photographs."

2 **Gumpoldskirchner:** bekannter Wein aus Gumpoldskirchen, Bezirk Mödling (Niederösterreich).
10 **toilet-stall:** Toilettenabteil.
13 **revolting:** widerwärtig.
13 f. **to expose o.s.:** sich zur Schau stellen; sich entblößen.
14 **passerby:** Vorübergehende(r).
15 **ankle:** (Fuß-)Knöchel.
20 **Schloss Katzelsdorf:** im Bezirk Wiener Neustadt (Niederösterreich) gelegen, gegründet im 12. Jh.

"Well, *that's* why the Hungarian's dream upset her," Father said.

"Someone is riding a bike in the hall," Robo said. "I saw a wheel go by – under our door."

"Robo, go to sleep," Mother said.

"It went 'squeak squeak,'" Robo said.

"Good night, boys," said Father.

"If you can talk, we can talk," I said.

"Then talk to each other," Father said. "I'm talking to your mother."

"I want to go to sleep," Mother said. "I wish no one would talk."

We tried. Perhaps we slept. Then Robo whispered to me that he had to use the W.C.

"You know where it is," I said.

Robo went out the door, leaving it slightly open; I heard him walk down the corridor, brushing his hand along the wall. He was back very quickly.

"There's someone *in* the W.C.," he said.

"Wait for them to finish," I said.

"The light wasn't on," Robo said, "but I could still see under the door. Someone is in there, in the dark."

"I prefer the dark myself," I said.

But Robo insisted on telling me exactly what he'd seen. He said that under the door was a pair of *hands*.

6 **to squeak:** quietschen.
17 **to brush one's hand along s.th.:** mit der Hand an etwas entlangstreifen.

"Hands?" I said.

"Yes, where the feet should have been," Robo said; he claimed that there was a hand on either side of the toilet – instead of a foot.

"Get out of here, Robo!" I said.

"Please come see," he begged. I went down the hall with him but there was no one in the W.C. "They've gone," he said.

"Walked off on their hands, no doubt," I said. "Go pee. I'll wait for you."

He went into the W.C. and peed sadly in the dark. When we were almost back to our room together, a small dark man with the same kind of skin and clothes as the dream man who had angered Grandmother passed us in the hall. He winked at us, and smiled, I had to notice that he was walking on his hands.

"You see?" Robo whispered to me. We went into our room and shut the door.

"What is it?" Mother asked.

"A man walking on his hands," I said.

"A man *peeing* on his hands," Robo said.

"Class C," Father murmured in his sleep; Father often dreamed that he was making notes in the giant pad.

"We'll talk about it in the morning," Mother said.

10 **to pee** (coll.): pinkeln.
15 **to wink at s.o.:** jdm. zuzwinkern.

"He was probably just an acrobat who was showing off for you, because you're a kid," I told Robo.

"How did he know I was a kid when he was in the W.C.?" Robo asked me.

"Go to *sleep*," Mother whispered.

Then we heard Grandmother scream down the hall.

Mother put on her pretty green dressing gown; Father put on his bathrobe and glasses. I pulled on a pair of pants, over my pajamas. Robo was in the hall first. We saw the light coming from under the W.C. door. Grandmother was screaming rhythmically in there.

"Here we are!" I called to her.

"Mother, what is it?" my mother asked.

We gathered in the broad slot of light. We could see Grandmother's mauve slippers and her porcelain-white ankles under the door. She stopped screaming. "I heard whispers when I was in my bed," she said.

"It was Robo and me," I told her.

"Then, when everyone seemed to have gone, I came into the W.C.," Johanna said. "I left the light

8 **dressing gown:** Morgenmantel.
9 **bathrobe:** Bademantel.
10 **pajamas** (pl.): Schlafanzug (BE *pyjamas*).
16 **to gather:** sich versammeln.
**slot:** Schlitz, Streifen, Stelle.
17 **mauve:** malvenfarbig (blasslila).
**slippers:** Hausschuhe, Pantoffeln.

*off.* I was *very* quiet," she told us. "Then I saw and heard the wheel."

"The *wheel?*" Father asked.

"A wheel went by the door a few times," Grandmother said. "It rolled by and came back and rolled by again."

Father made his fingers roll like wheels alongside his head; he made a face at Mother. "Somebody needs a new set of wheels," he whispered, but Mother looked crossly at him.

"I turned on the light," Grandmother said, "and the wheel went away."

"I told you there was a bike in the hall," said Robo.

"Shut up, Robo," Father said.

"No, it was not a bicycle," Grandmother said. "There was only one wheel."

Father was making his hands go crazy beside his head. "She's got a wheel or two *missing*," he hissed at my mother, but she cuffed him and knocked his glasses askew on his face.

"Then someone came and looked *under* the door," Grandmother said, "and *that* is when I screamed."

"Someone?" said Father.

7 f. **alongside:** neben.
19 **to hiss:** zischen.
20 **to cuff s.o.:** jdm. einen Klaps geben.
21 **askew:** schief.

"I saw his hands, a man's hands – there was hair on his knuckles," Grandmother said. "His hands were on the rug right outside the door. He must have been looking *up* at me."

"No, Grandmother," I said. "I think he was just standing out here on his hands."

"Don't be fresh," my mother said.

"But we saw a man walking on his hands," Robo said.

"You did *not*," Father said.

"We *did*," I said.

"We're going to wake everyone up," Mother cautioned us.

The toilet flushed and Grandmother shuffled out the door with only a little of her former dignity intact. She was wearing a gown over a gown over a gown; her neck was very long and her face was creamed white. Grandmother looked like a troubled goose. "He was evil and vile," she said to us. "He knew terrible magic."

"The man who looked at you?" Mother asked.

"That man who told my *dream*," Grandmother

2 **knuckles** (pl.): (Finger-)Knöchel.
7 **fresh:** frech.
13 **to caution:** warnen.
14 **to shuffle:** schlurfen.
16 **gown:** Kleidungsstück.
19 **evil:** böse.
**vile:** scheußlich, gemein.
20 **magic:** Zauberei.

said. Now a tear made its way through her furrows of face cream. "That was *my* dream," she said, "and he told everyone. It is unspeakable that he even *knew* it," she hissed to us. "*My* dream – of Charlemagne's horses and soldiers – I am the only one who should know it. I had that dream before you were born," she told Mother. "And that vile evil magic man told my dream as if it were *news.*

I never even told your father all there was to that dream. I was never sure that it *was* a dream. And now there are men on their hands, and their knuckles are hairy, and there are magic wheels. I want the boys to sleep with *me*."

So that was how Robo and I came to share the large family room, far away from the W.C., with Grandmother, who lay on my mother's and father's pillows with her creamed face shining like the face of a wet ghost. Robo lay awake watching her. I do not think Johanna slept very well; I imagine she was dreaming her dream of death again – reliving the last winter of Charlemagne's cold soldiers with their strange metal clothes covered with frost and their armor frozen shut.

When it was obvious that I had to go to the W.C., Robo's round, bright eyes followed me to the door.

There was someone in the W.C. There was no

1 **furrow:** Furche.
23 **frozen shut:** festgefroren.

light shining from under the door, but there was a unicycle parked against the wall outside. Its rider sat in the dark W.C.; the toilet was flushing over and over again – like a child, the unicyclist was not giving the tank time to refill.

I went closer to the gap under the W.C. door, but the occupant was not standing on his or her hands. I saw what were clearly feet, in almost the expected position, but the feet did not touch the floor; their soles tilted up to me – dark, bruise-colored pads. They were *huge* feet attached to short, furry shins. They were a *bear's* feet, only there were no claws. A bear's claws are not retractable, like a cat's; if a bear had claws, you would see them. Here, then, was an imposter in a bear suit, or a declawed bear. A domestic bear, perhaps. At least – by its presence in the W.C. – a *housebroken* bear. For by its smell I could tell it was no man in a bear suit; it was all bear. It was real bear.

2 **unicycle:** Einrad.
6 **gap:** Spalt, Lücke.
7 **occupant:** Benutzer(in) (einer Toilette).
10 **to tilt s.th. up:** etwas senkrecht stellen.
**bruise-colored pads:** etwa: blau unterlaufene Wülste.
11 **furry:** pelzig.
**shin:** Schienbein.
12 **claw:** Kralle.
13 **retractable:** einziehbar.
15 **imposter:** Schwindler.
**declawed:** ohne Krallen.
17 **housebroken:** stubenrein.

I backed into the door of Grandmother's former room, behind which my father lurked, waiting for further disturbances. He snapped open the door and I fell inside, frightening us both. Mother sat up in bed and pulled the feather quilt over her head. "Got him!" Father cried, dropping down on me. The floor trembled; the bear's unicycle slipped against the wall and fell into the door of the W.C., out of which the bear suddenly shambled, stumbling over its unicycle and lunging for its balance. Worriedly, it stared across the hall, through the open door, at Father sitting on my chest. It picked up the unicycle in its front paws. "*Grauf?*" said the bear. Father slammed the door.

Down the hall we heard a woman call, "Where are you, Duna?"

"*Harf!*" the bear said.

Father and I heard the woman come closer. She said, "Oh, Duna, practicing again? Always practicing! But it's better in the daytime." The bear said nothing. Father opened the door.

"Don't let anyone else in," Mother said, still under the featherbed.

2 **to lurk:** auf der Lauer liegen, lauern.
3 **disturbance:** Störung, Belästigung.
5 **feather quilt:** (gestepptes) Federbett, Steppdecke.
9 **to shamble:** watscheln, schlurfen.
10 **to lunge for one's balance:** die Balance zu finden versuchen.
13 **paw:** Tatze.
14 **to slam the door:** die Tür zuknallen.

In the hall a pretty, aging woman stood beside the bear, who now balanced in place on its unicycle, one huge paw on the woman's shoulder. She wore a vivid red turban and a long wrap-around dress that resembled a curtain. Perched on her high bosom was a necklace strung with bear claws; her earrings touched the shoulder of her curtain-dress and her other, bare shoulder where my father and I stared at her fetching mole. "Good evening," she said to Father. "I'm sorry if we've disturbed you. Duna is forbidden to practice at night – but he loves his work."

The bear muttered, pedaling away from the woman. The bear had very good balance but he was careless; he brushed against the walls of the hall and touched the photographs of the speed-skating teams with his paws. The woman, bowing away from Father, went after the bear calling, "Du-

2 **in place:** auf der Stelle.
4 **vivid:** in lebhaften Farben, bunt.
4f. **wrap-around dress:** Wickelkleid.
5 **to be perched:** (fig.) sitzen, thronen.
6 **necklace:** (Hals-)Kette.
**strung with bear claws:** mit aufgefädelten Bärenkrallen (*to string:* auffädeln, aufziehen).
7 **curtain-dress:** Bezug auf das üppig wallende Gewand von Scarlett O'Hara (dargestellt von Vivien Leigh) in dem Film *Gone with the Wind* (1939) nach dem gleichnamigen Roman (1936) von Margaret Mitchell.
9 **fetching:** (fig.) anziehend.
**mole:** Leberfleck.

na, Duna," and straightening the photographs as she followed him down the hall.

"*Duna* is the Hungarian word for the Danube," Father told me. "That bear is named after our beloved *Donau.*" Sometimes it seemed to surprise my family that the Hungarians could love a river, too.

"Is the bear a *real* bear?" Mother asked – still under the featherbed – but I left Father to explain it all to her. I knew that in the morning Herr Theobald would have much to explain, and I would hear everything reviewed at that time.

I went across the hall to the W.C. My task there was hurried by the bear's lingering odor, and by my suspicion of bear hair on everything; it was only my suspicion, though, for the bear had left everything quite tidy – or at least neat for a bear.

"I saw the bear," I whispered to Robo, back in our room, but Robo had crept into Grandmother's bed and had fallen asleep beside her. Old Johanna was awake, however.

"I saw fewer and fewer soldiers," she said. "The last time they came there were only nine of them. Everyone looked so hungry; they must have eaten the extra horses. It was so cold. Of course I wanted

1 **to straighten:** gerade richten.
3 **Danube:** Donau.
14 **to linger:** bleiben, verweilen; hier: in der Luft hängen.
**odor:** Geruch.
17 **neat:** sauber, ordentlich.

to help them! But we weren't alive at the same time; how could I help them if I wasn't even born? Of course I knew they would die! But it took such a long time.

The last time they came, the fountain was frozen. They used their swords and their long pikes to break the ice into chunks. They built a fire and melted the ice in a pot. They took bones from their saddlebags – bones of all kinds – and threw them in the soup. It must have been a very thin broth because the bones had long ago been gnawed clean. I don't know what bones they were. Rabbits, I suppose, and maybe a deer or a wild boar. Maybe the extra horses. I do not choose to think," said Grandmother, "that they were the bones of the missing soldiers."

"Go to sleep, Grandmother," I said.

"Don't worry about the bear," she said.

In the breakfast room of the Pension Grillparzer we confronted Herr Theobald with the menagerie of his other guests who had disrupted our evening.

6 **pike:** Pike (mittelalterliche Stoßwaffe aus einem Schaft mit Eisenspitze bestehend).
7 **chunk:** Stück.
10 **broth:** (dünne) Suppe.
11 **to gnaw:** nagen.
13 **boar:** Eber.
20 **menagerie** (iron.): (bunte) Gesellschaft.
21 **to disrupt:** stören, sprengen; hier: völlig durcheinanderbringen.

I knew that (as never before) my father was planning to reveal himself as a Tourist Bureau spy.

"Men walking about on their hands," said Father.

"Men looking under the door of the W.C.," said Grandmother.

"*That* man," I said, and pointed to the small, sulking fellow at the corner table, seated for breakfast with his cohorts – the dream man and the Hungarian singer.

"He does it for a living," Herr Theobald told us, and as if to demonstrate that this was so, the man who stood on his hands began to stand on his hands.

"Make him stop that," Father said. "We know he can do it."

"But did you know that he can't do it any other way?" the dream man asked suddenly. "Did you know that his legs were useless? He has no shinbones. It is *wonderful* that he can walk on his hands! Otherwise, he wouldn't walk at all." The man, although it was clearly hard to do while standing on his hands, nodded his head.

"Please sit down," Mother said.

"It is perfectly all right to be crippled," Grand-

8 **to sulk:** schmollen.
9 **cohorts:** Leute, Truppe.
19 f. **shinbone:** Schienbeinknochen.
25 **crippled:** verkrüppelt.

mother said, boldly. "But *you* are evil," she told the dream man. "You know things you have no right to know. He knew my *dream*," she told Herr Theobald, as if she were reporting a theft from her room.

"He is a *little* evil, I know," Theobald admitted. "But not usually! And he behaves better and better. He can't help what he knows."

"I was just trying to straighten you out," the dream man told Grandmother. "I thought it would do you good. Your husband has been dead quite a while, after all, and it's about time you stopped making so much of that dream. You're not the only person who's had such a dream."

"Stop it," Grandmother said.

"Well, you ought to know," said the dream man.

"No, be quiet, please," Herr Theobald told him.

"I am from the Tourist Bureau," Father announced, probably because he couldn't think of anything else to say.

"Oh my God shit!" Herr Theobald said.

"It's not Theobald's fault," said the singer. "It's *our* fault. He's nice to put up with us, though it costs him his reputation."

"They married my sister," Theobald told us. "They are *family*, you see. What can I do?"

"'They' married your sister?" Mother said.

4 **theft:** Diebstahl.
8 **to straighten s.o. out:** jdn. zur Einsicht bringen, aufklären.
22 **to put up with s.o.:** jdn. dulden.

"Well, she married *me* first," said the dream man.

"And then she heard *me* sing!" the singer said.

"She's never been married to the *other* one," Theobald said, and everyone looked apologetically toward the man who could only walk on his hands.

Theobald said, "They were once a circus art, but politics got them in trouble."

"We were the best in Hungary," said the singer. "You ever hear of the Circus Szolnok?"

"No, I'm afraid not," Father said, seriously.

"We played in Miskolc, in Szeged, in Debrecen," said the dream man.

"*Twice* in Szeged," the singer said.

"We would have made it to Budapest if it hadn't been for the Russians," said the man who walked on his hands.

"Yes, it was the Russians who removed his shinbones!" said the dream man.

"Tell the truth," the singer said. "He was *born* without shinbones. But it's true that we couldn't get along with the Russians."

"They tried to jail the bear," said the dream man.

"Tell the truth," Theobald said.

"We rescued his sister from them," said the man who walked on his hands.

4f. **apologetically:** entschuldigend.

12 **Miskolc / Szeged / Debrecen:** Großstädte in der Osthälfte Ungarns.

"So of course I must put them up," said Herr Theobald, "and they work as hard as they can. But who's interested in their act in this country? It's a Hungarian thing. There's no *tradition* of bears on unicycles here," Theobald told us. "And the damn dreams mean nothing to us Viennese."

"Tell the truth," said the dream man. "It is because I have told the wrong dreams. We worked a nightclub on the Kärntnerstrasse, but then we got banned."

"You should never have told *that* dream," the singer said gravely.

"Well, it was your wife's responsibility, too!" the dream man said.

"She was *your* wife, then," the singer said.

"Please stop it," Theobald begged.

"We get to do the balls for children's diseases," the dream man said. "And some of the state hospitals – especially at Christmas."

"If you would only do more with the bear," Herr Theobald advised them.

"Speak to your sister about that," said the singer. "It's *her* bear – she's trained him, she's let him get lazy and sloppy and full of bad habits."

12 **gravely:** ernst, vieldeutig.
17 **to do the balls for s.th.:** bei Veranstaltungen auftreten zugunsten von etwas.
21 **to advise:** raten.
24 **sloppy** (coll.): schlampig.

"He is the only one of you who never makes fun of me," said the man who could only walk on his hands.

"I would like to leave all this," Grandmother said. "This is, for me, an awful experience."

"Please, dear lady," Herr Theobald said, "we only wanted to show you that we meant no offense. These are hard times. I need the B rating to attract more tourists, and I can't – in my heart – throw out the Circus Szolnok."

"*In his heart*, my ass!" said the dream man. "He's afraid of his sister. He wouldn't dream of throwing us out."

"If he dreamed it, you would know it!" cried the man on his hands.

"I am afraid of the *bear*," Herr Theobald said. "It does everything she tells it to do."

"Say 'he,' not 'it,'" said the man on his hands. "He is a fine bear, and he never hurt anybody. He has no claws, you know perfectly well – and very few teeth, either."

"The poor thing has a terribly hard time eating," Herr Theobald admitted. "He is quite old, and he's messy."

Over my father's shoulder, I saw him write in the

7 **we meant no offense:** wir haben es nicht böse gemeint.
11 **my ass!** (coll.): du meine Güte!
24 **messy:** schmutzig, unsauber.

giant pad: "A depressed bear and an unemployed circus. This family is centered on the sister."

At that moment out on the sidewalk, we could see her tending to the bear. It was early morning and the street was not especially busy. By law, of course, she had the bear on a leash, but it was a token control. In her startling red turban the woman walked up and down the sidewalk, following the lazy movements of the bear on his unicycle. The animal pedaled easily from parking meter to parking meter, sometimes leaning a paw on the meter as he turned. He was very talented on the unicycle, you could tell, but you could also tell that the unicycle was a dead end for him. You could see that the bear felt he could go no further with unicycling.

"She should bring him off the street now," Herr Theobald fretted. "The people in the pastry shop next door complain to me," he told us. "They say the bear drives their customers away."

1 **unemployed:** ohne Arbeit, arbeitslos.
2 **to be centered on s.o.:** auf jdn. ausgerichtet sein.
3 **sidewalk:** Bürgersteig.
4 **to tend to s.o.:** sich um jdn. kümmern.
6 **leash:** Leine.
6f. **to be a token control:** bloßer Schein sein.
7 **startling:** auffallend, Aufsehen erregend.
10 **parking meter:** Parkuhr.
14 **dead end:** Sackgasse.
18 **to fret:** sich aufregen, gereizt bemerken.

"That bear makes the customers *come!*" said the man on his hands.

"It makes some people come, it turns some away," said the dream man. He was suddenly somber, as if his profundity had depressed him.

But we had been so taken up with the antics of the Circus Szolnok that we had neglected old Johanna. When my mother saw that Grandmother was quietly crying, she told me to bring the car around.

"It's been too much for her," my father whispered to Theobald. The Circus Szolnok looked ashamed of themselves.

Outside on the sidewalk the bear pedaled up to me and handed me the keys; the car was parked at the curb. "Not everyone likes to be given the keys in that fashion," Herr Theobald told his sister.

"Oh, I thought he'd rather like it," she said, rumpling my hair. She was as appealing as a barmaid, which is to say that she was more appealing at night; in the daylight I could see that she was older than her brother, and older than her husbands too – and in time, I imagined, she would cease being

4f. **somber:** melancholisch.
5 **profundity:** Tiefsinnigkeit.
6 **antics:** Mätzchen, Possen.
16 **curb:** Bordstein.
19 **appealing:** reizvoll.
23 **in time:** mit der Zeit.
**to cease:** aufhören.

lover and sister to them, respectively, and become a mother to them all. She was already a mother to the bear.

"Come over here," she said to him. He pedaled listlessly in place on his unicycle, holding on to a parking meter for support. He licked the little glass face of the meter. She tugged his leash. He stared at her. She tugged again. Insolently, the bear began to pedal – first one way, then the next. It was as if he took interest, seeing that he had an audience. He began to show off.

"Don't try anything," the sister said to him, but the bear pedaled faster and faster, going forward, going backward, angling sharply and veering among the parking meters; the sister had to let go of the leash. "Duna, stop it!" she cried, but the bear was out of control. He let the wheel roll too close to the curb and the unicycle pitched him hard into the fender of a parked car. He sat on the sidewalk with the unicycle beside him; you could tell that he hadn't injured himself, but he looked very embarrassed and nobody laughed. "Oh, Duna,"

1 **respectively:** in dieser Reihenfolge.
5 **listlessly:** lustlos.
7 **to tug s.th.:** an etwas zerren, (heftig) ziehen.
8 **insolently:** unverschämt, frech.
14 **to angle:** abbiegen.
**to veer:** sich drehen; in Schlangenlinien fahren.
18 **to pitch:** schleudern.
19 **fender:** Schutzblech.
22 **embarrassed:** verlegen.

the sister said, scoldingly, but she went over and crouched beside him at the curb. "Duna, Duna," she reproved him, gently. He shook his big head; he would not look at her. There was some saliva strung on the fur near his mouth and she wiped this away with her hand. He pushed her hand away with his paw.

"Come back again!" cried Herr Theobald, miserably, as we got into our car.

Mother sat in the car with her eyes closed and her fingers massaging her temples; this way she seemed to hear nothing we said. She claimed it was her only defense against traveling with such a contentious family.

I did not want to report on the usual business concerning the care of the car, but I saw that Father was trying to maintain order and calm; he had the giant pad spread on his lap as if we'd just completed a routine investigation. "What does the gauge tell us?" he asked.

"Someone put thirty-five kilometers on it," I said.

"That terrible bear has been in here," Grandmother said. "There are hairs from the beast on the back seat, and I can *smell* him."

1 **scoldingly:** vorwurfsvoll.
2 **to crouch:** kauern, hocken.
3 **to reprove:** tadeln.
4 **saliva:** Speichel.
11 **temple:** Schläfe.
13f. **contentious:** streitsüchtig.

"I don't smell anything," Father said.

"And the perfume of that gypsy in the turban," Grandmother said. "It is hovering near the ceiling of the car." Father and I sniffed. Mother continued to massage her temples.

On the floor by the brakes and clutch pedals I saw several of the mint-green toothpicks that the Hungarian singer was in the habit of wearing like a scar at the corner of his mouth. I didn't mention them. It was enough to imagine them all – out on the town, in our car. The singing driver, the man on his hands beside him – waving out the window with his feet. And in back, separating the dream man from his former wife – his great head brushing the upholstered roof, his mauling paws relaxed in his large lap – the old bear slouched like a benign drunk.

"Those poor people," Mother said, her eyes still closed.

"Liars and criminals," Grandmother said. "Mystics and refugees and broken-down animals."

3 **to hover:** schweben.
6 **clutch pedal:** Kupplungspedal.
7 **mint-green:** türkisgrün (*mint:* Minze).
**toothpick:** Zahnstocher.
8 **scar:** Narbe.
14 **upholstered:** gepolstert.
15 **to maul:** übel zurichten.
16 **to slouch:** sich lümmeln.
**benign:** gutartig, gutmütig.
19f. **mystic:** Schwärmer; Geheimniskrämer.
20 **refugee:** Flüchtling.

"They were trying hard," Father said, "but they weren't coming up with the prizes."

"Better off in a zoo," said Grandmother.

"I had a good time," Robo said.

"It's hard to break out of Class C," I said.

"They have fallen past Z," said old Johanna. "They have disappeared from the human alphabet."

"I think this calls for a letter," Mother said.

But Father raised his hand – as if he were going to bless us – and we were quiet. He was writing in the giant pad and wished to be undisturbed. His face was stern. I knew that Grandmother felt confident of his verdict. Mother knew it was useless to argue. Robo was already bored. I steered us off through the tiny streets; I took Spiegelgasse to Lobkowitzplatz. Spiegelgasse is so narrow that you can see the reflection of your own car in the windows of the shops you pass, and I felt our movement through Vienna was superimposed (like that) – like a trick with a movie camera, as if we made a fairy-tale journey through a toy city.

When Grandmother was asleep in the car, Mother said, "I don't suppose that in this case a change in the classification will matter very much, one way or another."

2 **to come up with the prizes:** etwa: mit der Spitze Schritt halten.
10 **to bless:** segnen.
12 **stern:** streng.
13 **verdict:** Urteil.
19 **to superimpose:** einblenden (Film), (Bild) aufkopieren.

"No," Father said, "not much at all." He was right about that, though it would be years until I saw the Pension Grillparzer again.

When Grandmother died, rather suddenly and in her sleep, Mother announced that she was tired of traveling. The real reason, however, was that she began to find herself plagued by Grandmother's dream. "The horses are so thin," she told me once. "I mean, I always knew they would be thin, but not *this* thin. And the soldiers – I knew they were miserable," she said, "but not *that* miserable."

Father resigned from the Tourist Bureau and found a job with a local detective agency specializing in hotels and department stores. It was a satisfactory job for him, though he refused to work during the Christmas season – when, he said, some people ought to be allowed to steal a little.

My parents seemed to me to relax as they got older, and I really felt they were fairly happy near the end. I know that the strength of Grandmother's dream was dimmed by the *real* world, and specifically by what happened to Robo. He went to a private school and was well liked there, but he was killed by a homemade bomb in his first year at the university. He was not even "political." In his last

7 **to plague s.o.:** jdn. plagen, quälen, verfolgen.
12 **to resign from s.th.:** bei etwas kündigen.
24 **homemade:** selbst gebastelt.

letter to my parents he wrote: "The self-seriousness of the radical factions among the students is much overrated. And the food is execrable." Then Robo went to his history class, and his classroom was blown apart.

It was after my parents died that I gave up smoking and took up traveling again. I took my second wife back to the Pension Grillparzer. With my first wife, I never got as far as Vienna.

The Grillparzer had not kept Father's B rating very long, and it had fallen from the ratings altogether by the time I returned to it. Herr Theobald's sister was in charge of the place. Gone was her tart appeal and in its place was the sexless cynicism of some maiden aunts. She was shapeless and her hair was dyed a sort of bronze, so that her head resembled one of those copper scouring pads that you use on a pot. She did not remember me and was suspicious of my questions. Because I appeared to know so much about her past associates, she probably knew I was with the police.

1 f. **the self-seriousness of the radical factions:** die Art, wie ernst sich die rakidalen Gruppen nehmen.
3 **to overrate:** überschätzen.
**execrable:** abscheulich.
13 **tart** (slang): Flittchen.
15 **maiden:** altjüngferlich.
16 **to dye:** färben.
17 **copper scouring pad:** kupferfarbener Topfreiniger aus Stahlwolle.
20 **associate:** Gefährte.

The Hungarian singer had gone away – another woman thrilled by his voice. The dream man had been *taken* away – to an institution. His own dreams had turned to nightmares and he'd awakened the pension each night with his horrifying howls. His removal from the seedy premises, said Herr Theobald's sister, was almost simultaneous with the loss of the Grillparzer's B rating.

Herr Theobald was dead. He had dropped down clutching his heart in the hall, where he ventured one night to investigate what he thought was a prowler. It was only Duna, the malcontent bear, who was dressed in the dream man's pin-striped suit. Why Theobald's sister had dressed the bear in this fashion was not explained to me, but the shock of the sullen animal unicycling in the lunatic's left-behind clothes had been enough to scare Herr Theobald to death.

2 **thrilled:** fasziniert, begeistert.
3 **institution:** Anstalt (für geistig Verwirrte).
4 **nightmare:** Albtraum.
5 **horrifying:** entsetzlich.
6 **howl:** Geheul, Gebrüll.
**seedy:** verwahrlost, heruntergekommen.
**premises** (pl.): Grundstück, Haus.
7 **simultaneous:** gleichzeitig.
10 **to clutch:** packen, umklammern.
12 **prowler:** Herumtreiber.
**malcontent:** unzufrieden.
16 **sullen:** verdrossen.
**lunatic:** Verrückter.
17 f. **to scare s.o. to death:** jdn. zu Tode erschrecken.

The man who could only walk on his hands had also fallen into the gravest trouble. His wristwatch snagged on a tine of an escalator and he was suddenly unable to hop off; his necktie, which he rarely wore because it dragged on the ground when he walked on his hands, was drawn under the step-off grate at the end of the escalator – where he was strangled. Behind him a line of people formed – marching in place by taking one step back and allowing the escalator to carry them forward, then taking another step back. It was quite a while before anyone got up the nerve to step over him. The world has many unintentionally cruel mechanisms that are not designed for people who walk on their hands.

After that, Theobald's sister told me, the Pension Grillparzer went from Class C to much worse. As the burden of management fell more heavily on her, she had less time for Duna and the bear grew senile and indecent in his habits. Once he bullied a

2 **grave:** schwer, tief.
3 **to snag:** sich verhaken.
**tine:** Zacke.
**escalator:** Rolltreppe.
4 **necktie:** Krawatte.
5 **to drag:** schleifen.
6f. **step-off grate:** Abtrittstufe (einer Rolltreppe).
8 **to strangle:** erdrosseln.
13 **unintentionally:** unabsichtlich.
20 **indecent:** unanständig.
**to bully:** drangsalieren; hier: jagen.

mailman down a marble staircase at such a ferocious pace that the man fell and broke his hip: the attack was reported and an old city ordinance forbidding unrestrained animals in places open to the public was enforced. Duna was outlawed at the Pension Grillparzer.

For a while, Theobald's sister kept the bear in a cage in the courtyard of the building, but he was taunted by dogs and children, and food (and worse) was dropped into his cage from the apartments that faced the courtyard. He grew unbearlike and devious – only pretending to sleep – and he ate most of someone's cat. Then he was poisoned twice and became afraid to eat anything in this perilous environment. There was no alternative but to donate him to the Schönbrunn Zoo, but there was even some doubt as to his acceptability. He was toothless and

1 **marble:** Marmor.
1 f. **ferocious pace:** scharfes Tempo.
2 **hip:** Hüfte.
3 **ordinance:** Verordnung.
4 **unrestrained:** unkontrolliert; hier: frei herumlaufend.
5 **to enforce:** (Vorschrift) durchsetzen.
**to be outlawed:** geächtet werden; hier: Hausverbot erhalten.
9 **to taunt:** verhöhnen, verspotten.
11 f. **devious:** verschlagen.
14 **perilous:** gefährlich.
14 f. **environment:** Milieu, Umgebung.
15 **to donate:** schenken.
16 **Schönbrunn Zoo:** Wiener Tiergarten im Park des Schlosses Schönbrunn, gegründet 1752.
17 **acceptability:** Annehmbarkeit.

ill, perhaps contagious, and his long history of having been treated as a human being did not prepare him for the gentler routine of zoo life.

His outdoor sleeping quarters in the courtyard of the Grillparzer had inflamed his rheumatism, and even his one talent, unicycling, was irretrievable. When he first tried it in the zoo, he fell. Someone laughed. Once anyone laughed at something Duna did, Theobald's sister explained, Duna would never do that thing again. He became, at last, a kind of charity case at Schönbrunn, where he died a short two months after he'd taken up his new lodgings. In the opinion of Theobald's sister, Duna died of mortification – the result of a rash that spread over his great chest, which then had to be shaved. A shaved bear, one zoo official said, is embarrassed to death.

In the cold courtyard of the building I looked in the bear's empty cage. The birds hadn't left a fruit seed, but in a corner of his cage was a looming mound of the bear's ossified droppings – as void of

1 **contagious:** ansteckend.
5 **to inflame:** entzünden; hier: zum Ausbruch bringen.
6 f. **irretrievable:** nicht zurückzugewinnen, endgültig verloren.
11 **charity case:** Fall mildtätiger Nächstenliebe.
14 **mortification:** Kränkung.
**rash:** Hautausschlag.
20 **to loom:** sich auftürmen, aufragen.
21 **mound:** Hügel, Haufen.
**ossified:** verknöchert; hier: vertrocknet.
21 f. **void of life:** ohne jedes Leben.

life, and even odor, as the corpses captured by the holocaust at Pompeii. I couldn't help thinking of Robo; of the bear, there were more remains.

In the car I was further depressed to notice that not one kilometer had been added to the gauge, not one kilometer had been driven in secret. There was no one around to take liberties anymore.

"When we're a safe distance away from your precious Pension Grillparzer," my second wife said to me, "I'd like you to tell me why you brought me to such a shabby place."

"It's a long story," I admitted.

I was thinking I had noticed a curious lack of either enthusiasm or bitterness in the account of the world by Theobald's sister. There was in her story the flatness one associates with a storyteller who is accepting of unhappy endings, as if her life and her companions had never been exotic to *her* – as if they had always been staging a ludicrous and doomed effort at reclassification.

2 **Pompeii:** Stadt im Golf von Neapel, im Jahr 79 n.Ch. bei einem Ausbruch des Vesuvs völlig unter Asche begraben, inzwischen größtenteils ausgegraben und zugänglich als weltbekanntes Museum des Lebens in der Antike.
3 **remains:** Überreste.
7 **to take liberties:** sich (unerlaubt) Freiheiten herausnehmen.
14 **account:** Darstellung.
19 **to stage:** inszenieren, veranstalten, unternehmen.
**ludicrous:** lächerlich, absurd.
20 **doomed:** zum Scheitern verurteilt.

## Author's Notes

Readers of *The World According to Garp* may remember that "The Pension Grillparzer" is T. S. Garp's first short story, and the first evidence in the novel of Garp's abilities as a young writer. Indeed, he is a *very* young writer when he is supposed to have written "Grillparzer" – he is only 19. The late Henry Robbins, who was a dear friend and the editor of *The World According to Garp*, told me that the story was much too good for a 19-year-old to have written it.

I argued that I wanted to make a point about Garp, which is a point I have made about many American writers: the first thing they write is the best thing they *ever* write – in Garp's case, it was all downhill after "Grillparzer". But Henry insisted that I had made "Grillparzer" seem too easy to write; it was Henry's suggestion that, for the credibility of the novel, I break up the story – that I have Garp begin it and get stuck in it and put it aside. Garp takes up the story and finishes it only after an interval of several months; the death of a friend, a Viennese prostitute, is the real-life episode that informs the young author about the end of his story.

4 **evidence:** Beweis, Anzeichen.
16 **downhill:** ganz einfach.
18f. **credibility:** Glaubwürdigkeit.

I agreed with Henry, and so "The Pension Grillparzer" was divided; readers who read it in the novel read it in two parts. I knew Henry was right, but I hated breaking up the story, which was originally published, two years before *The World According to Garp*, in *Antaeus* (Winter 1976); it won a Pushcart Prize – the Best of the Small Presses – but I suspect that most readers saw it first in *Garp*, in its divided form. That is why I wanted to publish it here – for the first time, for many readers, *whole*; of one piece.

In the middle of the story, when Garp gets "stuck" and stops writing, Garp ponders the following: "But what did they mean? That dream and those desperate entertainers, and what would happen to them all – everything had to connect. What sort of explanation would be natural? What sort of ending might make them all part of the same world?"

What made "The Pension Grillparzer" special to me (it is my favorite among my short stories) was both the grandmother's dream and the epilogue – everything *does* "connect." The "ludicrous and doomed effort at reclassification" is a foreshadow of the "terminal cases" theme of the novel, which has its own epilogue – I like epilogues, as anyone who's read my novels knows. The younger brother

13 **to ponder s.th.:** über etwas nachdenken.
22 **epilogue:** Epilog, Nachwort.

blown up in a history class, the innkeeper frightened to death by the bear "unicycling in the lunatic's left-behind clothes" – the bear himself is "embarrassed to death" – and especially the man who could only walk on his hands, strangled by his necktie on an escalator ... these calamities foreshadow some of the violent ends that my characters will meet, not only in *Garp* but in later novels; these are the unlikely disasters that many book reviewers have called my penchant for the bizarre.

But, according to Henry Robbins – and I believed him; I believe him to this day – the *most* bizarre element in *The World According to Garp* is that a 19-year-old could have written "The Pension Grillparzer." Not one book reviewer ever made mention of that.

At the time *I* wrote "Grillparzer," I had already written three-and-a-half novels; I was 34. And I already knew I was a novelist, not a short-story writer; yet I never worked as hard on a short story, before or since, because I wanted the readers of *The World According to Garp* to know that T. S. Garp was a good writer.

6 **calamity:** Unglück.
6f. **to foreshadow s.th.:** auf etwas hindeuten, etwas ahnen lassen.
10 **penchant:** Hang, Neigung.

# Editorische Notiz

Der englische Text folgt der Ausgabe: John Irving, *Trying to Save Piggy Sneed*, London: Black Swan, 1994, S. 157–187.

Das Glossar enthält alle Wörter, die nicht im *Thematischen Grund- und Aufbauwortschatz Englisch* von Gernot Häublein und Recs Jenkins (Stuttgart/Düsseldorf/Leipzig: Ernst Klett Verlag, 1993) verzeichnet sind. Dabei wird der Grundwortschatz in der Regel als bekannt vorausgesetzt; Wörter, die zum Aufbauwortschatz zählen, sind bei Bedarf erklärt. Damit sollte es Leserinnen und Lesern mit Englischkenntnissen ab der 10. Klasse selbst bei extensiver Lektüre möglich sein, die Erzählung ohne weiteren Gebrauch des Wörterbuches mit Freude und Spannung zu lesen.

Das Nachwort verfolgt das Ziel, dass über die Short Story ein Zugang zum Autor und seinen weiteren, fast ausschließlich wesentlich umfangreicheren Werken leicht erschlossen werden kann; es wird aber die eigenständige Auseinandersetzung mit Irving in keinem Fall ersetzen. Dazu bieten wiederum die selektiv angelegten bibliographischen Angaben eine Hilfe, wobei bewusst einige Internetseiten eingefügt sind, um auch bei fehlenden Zugriffsmöglichkeiten auf Bibliotheken eine gezielte Recherche zu ermöglichen. Auf diese Weise kann der Band Schülern, Studenten und Lehrern die Vorbereitung und Erstellung von Studienarbeiten erleichtern und Hinweise auf Themenaspekte vermitteln, die auch in anderen Werken John Irvings anzutreffen sind.

Die »Author's Notes« werden als Selbstaussage Irvings zu seiner Kurzgeschichte hier zusätzlich abgedruckt und sind der von ihm völlig neu zusammengestellten, erweiterten Ausgabe der Sammlung *Trying to Save Piggy Sneed*, New York: Arcade Publishing, 1996, S. 266–268, entnommen.

*Im Glossar verwendete englische Abkürzungen*

| | |
|---|---|
| BE | British English |
| coll. | colloquial (umgangssprachlich) |
| fig. | figuratively (übertragen) |
| idiom. | idiomatic |
| iron. | ironical |
| o.s. | oneself |
| pej. | pejorative (abwertend) |
| pl. | plural |
| s.o. | someone |
| s.th. | something |

# Literaturhinweise

## *Werke*

Die Liste der Primärliteratur verweist hier auf die Originalausgaben. Soweit im Nachwort auf Irvings Romane Bezug genommen wird, sind die verwendeten Nachdrucke dort ausgewiesen. Alle Romane sind in deutscher Übersetzung und teilweise als Hörbücher erhältlich.

1. Romane

*Setting Free the Bears*, New York: Random House, 1968.

*The Water-Method Man*, New York: Random House, 1972.

*The 158-Pound Marriage*, New York: Random House, 1974.

*The World According to Garp*, New York: E.P. Dutton, 1978.

*The Hotel New Hampshire*, New York: E.P. Dutton, 1981.

*The Cider House Rules*, New York: W. Morrow, 1985.

*A Prayer for Own Meany*, New York: W. Morrow, 1989.

*A Son of the Circus*, New York: Random House, 1994.

*A Widow for One Year*, New York: Random House, 1998.

*The Fourth Hand*, New York: Random House, 2001.

*Until I Find You,* New York: Random House, 2000.

*Last Night in Twisted River*, London: Bloomsbury Publishing, 2009.

2. Sammelbände

*3 By Irving*, New York: Random House, 1980 (darin *Setting Free the Bears, The Water-Method Man, The 158-Pound Marriage*).

*Trying to Save Piggy Sneed*, London / Knopf Canada 1993 (darin sieben Kurzgeschichten und ein Essay).

*Trying to Save Piggy Sneed*, New York: Arcade Publishing, 1996 (darin »Trying to Save Piggy Sneed«, »The Imaginary Girlfriend«, S. 25–145, »My Dinner at the White House«, »Interior Space«, »Brennbar's Rant«, »The Pension Grillparzer«, S. 233–265, »Other People's Dreams«, »Weary Kingdom«, »Almost in Iowa«, »King of the Novel«, »Introduction to the Christmas Carol«, »Gunther Grass: King of the Toy Merchants«).

3. Drehbuch

*The Cider House Rules – A Screenplay*, New York: Hyperion, 1999. (Deutscher Filmtitel: *Gottes Werk und Teufels Beitrag*.)

Verfilmt wurden darüber hinaus sehr erfolgreich die Romane *The World According to Garp* mit Robin Williams in der Titelrolle, *The Hotel New Hampshire*, *A Widow for One Year* mit dem Titel *A Door in the Floor*, *A Prayer for Owen Meany* mit dem Titel *Simon Birch* (Drehbuch nicht vom Autor akzeptiert).

4. Kurzgeschichten

»A Winter Branch«, in: *Redbook* 126 (November 1965) S. 56f., 143–146.

»Weary Kingdom«, in: *The Boston Review* (Frühjahr/ Sommer 1968) S. 8–35.

»Lost in New York«, in: *Esquire* 79 (März 1973) S. 116f., 152.

»Almost in Iowa«, in: *Esquire* 80 (November 1973) S. 143–146, 224–229.

»Brennbar's Rant«, in: *Playboy* 21 (Dezember 1974) S. 4, 137, 304–307.

»Students: These Are Your Teachers«, in: *Esquire* 84 (September 1975) S. 68, 156–159.

»The Pension Grillparzer«, in: *Antaeus* (Winter 1976) S. 7–27.

»Vigilance«, in: *Ploughshares* 4 (1977) S. 103–117.

»Dog in the Alley«, »Child in the Sky«, in: *Esquire* 87 (Juni 1977) S. 108f., 158–162.

»Interior Space«, in: *Fiction* 6, Nr. 2 (1980) S. 26–58.

»A Bear Called State O'Maine«, in: *Rolling Stone* 20 (August 1981) S. 22–27, 50–55 (Auszug aus: *The Hotel New Hampshire*).

»The Foul Ball«, in: *New Yorker* 64 (Januar 1988) S. 28–40, 44–46, 50–52, 54–56 (Variation von *A Prayer for Owen Meany*).

»The Making of a Writer: Trying to Save Piggy Sneed«, in: *New York Times Book Review*, 22. August 1982, S. 3, 20–22.

5. Sonstige Schriften

»Best Seller: What Does It Really Mean?«, in: *Vogue* 169 (April 1969) S. 154–156.

»Neglected Books of the Twentieth Century«, in: *Antaeus* 27 (Herbst 1977) S. 131 f.

»Life After Graduation According to Garp«, in: *Esquire* 91 (27. März 1979) S. 53.

»Kurt Vonnegut and His Critics: The Aesthetics of Accessibility«, in: *New Republic* 181 (September 1979) S. 41 f.

»In Defense of Sentimentality«, in: *New York Times Book Review*, 25. November 1979, S. 3, 96.

»Getting Started: A Novelist Beginning a New Book Must Plan to Get the Reader Hooked – and Himself Involved«, in: *Publishers Weekly*, 24. Januar 1991, S. 2.

»Pornography and the New Puritans«, in: *New York Times Book Review*, 29. März 1992, S. 1, 24 f., 27.

*My Movie Business – A Memoir*, New York: Random House, 1999.

*The Imaginary Girlfriend – A Memoir*, New York: Random House, 2002 (vorab erschienen als Teil von *Trying to Save Piggy Sneed*, New York: Arcade Publishing, 1996).

Die Sammlung der Schriften und Manuskripte John Irvings befindet sich in der Bibliothek der Phillips Exeter Academy, Exeter, New Hampshire.

## *Interviews mit John Irving*


1. auf Englisch

Richard West, »John Irving's World After Garp«, in: *New York Magazine*, 14. August 1981, S. 29–32.

James Feron, »All About Writing, According to Irving«, in: *New York Times*, 29. November 1981, S. 4.

Larry McCaffery, »An Interview with John Irving«, in: *Contemporary Literature*, Bd. 23, University of Wisconsin Press (Winter 1982) S. 1–18.

Corby Kummer, »John Irving: Fascinated by Orphans«, in: *Book-of-the-Month-Club News*, Sommer 1985, S. 5.

Richard, Bernstein, »John Irving: 19th Century Novelist for These Times«, in: *New York Times*, 25. April 1989, C 13, C 17.

2. auf Deutsch

»Für Sex bezahlt man immer – Der Kämpfer«, in: *ZEIT-Magazin*, Nr. 7, 11. Februar 1999.

»Wenn Leute dich umbringen wollen, töte sie zuerst«, in: *Frankfurter Rundschau*, 26. Januar 2002.

»Ich war schon immer klüger«, in: *Der Spiegel*, 21. Januar 2002.

»Die einzige Waffe, die erlaubt ist«, in: *Frankfurter Allgemeine Zeitung*, 29. März 2003.

»Aufgetaucht aus der Vergangenheit«, in: *Stern*, 10. November 2005.

*Sekundärliteratur*


Braun, Hartmut, *Literatur als Zerrspiegel, Metafiktion in den Romanen von John Irving*, Osnabrück: Der Andere Verlag, 2004.

Campbell, Josie P., *John Irving, A Critical Companion*, Westport (Conn.) / London 1998.

Klinkowitz, Jerome, *Literary Subversions. New American Fiction and the Practice of Criticism,* Carbondale: Southern Illinois University Press, 1985.

Harter, Carol C. / Thompson, James R., *John Irving*, Boston: Twayne, 1986.

Miller, Gabriel, *John Irving,* New York: Frederick Ungar, 1982.

Reilly, Edward C., *Understanding John Irving*, Columbia: University of South Carolina Press, 1991.

– »A John Irving Bibliography«, in: *Bulletin of Bibliography* (März 1985) S. 12–18.

Ruppersburg, Hugh M., »John Irving«, in: J. E. Kibler (Hrsg.), *Dictionary of Literary Biography: American Novelists Since World War II*, 2nd Series, Detroit (Mich.): Gale Research Company, 1980, S. 153–161.

Sinic, Barbara, *Die sozialkritische Funktion des Grotesken, analysiert anhand der Romane von Vonnegut, Irving, Boyle, Grass, Rosendorfer und Widmer,* Frankfurt a. M.: Lang, 2003.

Weiß, Elke, *John Irving und die Kunst des Fabulierens*, Frankfurt a. M.: Lang, 2002.

*Internetseiten*

Academy of Achievement, Washington, »John Irving Biography«
www.achievement.org/autodoc/page/irv0bio-1

Arx, Ursula von, »Das erste Mal – John Irving, brauchen Sie den Erfolg?«, in: *Neue Zürcher Zeitung Folio* (Februar 2007)
www.nzzfolio.ch/www/d80bd71b-b264-4db4-afd0-277884b93470/showarticle/b0

Booksearch and Marketplace, Biblio.com, »John Irving«
www.biblio.com/authors/665/John_Irving_Biography.html

Ecker, Daniela, »John Irving, vorgestellt in der LESELUST«
www.die-leselust.de/autoren/irving_john.htm

Focus online, 27. Februar 2007, »John Irving, Meister der Erzählkunst«
www.focus.de/kultur/buecher/john-irving_aid_125401.html

Harrigan, Jane, »Becoming John Irving«, in: *University of New Hampshire Magazine Online* (2005)
http://unhmagazine.unh.edu/f05/johnirving.html

Herel, Suzanne, »John Irving (interviewed)«, in: *Mother Jones* (Mai/Juni 1997)
www.motherjones.com/arts/qa/1997/05/outspoken.html

»John Irving: Biography from Answers.com«
www.answers.com/topic/john-irving

Lewis, Leon, »John Irving«, The Literary Encyclopedia, 2005
www.litencyc.com/php/speople.php?rec=true&UID=2313

Norris, Gary, »A selective and excessive bibliography«
www.geocities.com/irvingophile/Home.html
Schnitzler, Meike, »Ich erzähl euch was, das wird euch die Hosen ausziehen«, in: Brigitte, 18. Januar 2006
www.Brigitte.de/kultur/buecher_cds/irving_portraet/
Smith, Joan, »The *Salon* Interview – John Irving«, 3. März 1997
www.salon.com/march97/interview2970303.html
Stark, Jeff, »The John Irving Rules«, in: Salon.com, 8. März 2000
http://archive.salon.com/ent/movies/int/2000/03/08/irving/
Swaim, Don, »Audio Interviews with John Irving, 1985 und 1989«, Ohio University
http://wiredforbooks.org/johnirving/
www.wikipedia.org/wiki/John_Irving [Hier gibt es zahlreiche weitere Links.]

Eine Übersicht zu den Irving-Büchern des New Yorker Verlags Random House und dessen Informationen zum Autor findet sich unter
www.randomhouse.com/randomhouse/authors/results.pperl?authorid=14109

# Nachwort

Er steht seit Jahrzehnten an der Spitze der Bestsellerlisten, hasst aber noch immer Rezensenten, Feuilletonisten und Literaturkritiker, die ihm und anderen Autoren seiner Meinung nach nicht gerecht werden, bezeichnet einen der bekanntesten deutschen Literaturkritiker in einem Interview unverblümt als »kulturloses Arschloch«, der sich nur mittels der Medien aufblasen könne, ist befreundet mit Günter Grass und vielen anderen Exponenten des Literaturbetriebs, zeichnet sich aus als Mensch und berühmter Autor mit Ecken und Kanten, geliebt von vielen, abgelehnt von anderen – John Irving.

## Einstimmung auf einen ungewöhnlichen Autor

Als 1978 der vierte Roman des jungen Autors John Irving, *The World According to Garp*, erscheint und in kurzer Zeit Millionenauflagen erreicht, kündigt das *Dictionary of Literary Biography* ziemlich überzeugt an, dass sein bisheriges Erzählwerk, lebendig, unterhaltend, ergreifend und ernsthaft, darauf hindeute, dass hier ein Stern am Himmel der amerikanischen Literaturszene aufgehe. Die Voraussage traf die tatsächliche Entwicklung in der Rückschau korrekt, ohne aber die Wucht der Wirkung jenes Autors auf Abermillionen Leser in der ganzen Welt während der folgenden Jahrzehnte vorausahnen zu können. Gleichwohl musste Irving rund zwanzig Jahre später in einem Interview für das Magazin *Salon* feststellen, dass Romanciers auf den Bestsellerlisten der *New York Times* offensichtlich gar keine Rolle mehr spielten und die »bestsellers« jener Listen alle »shit« seien, während das in Kanada, Deutschland, Frankreich und England viel besser aussehe und deshalb der größere Teil seiner Buchauflagen als Übersetzungen seine Leser finde; so seien von *A Son of the Circus* in Deutschland mehr Exemplare verkauft worden als in den USA und Kanada zusammen. Im gleichen Interview teilt der Autor mit, dass er keinen Wert lege auf die miserablen Buchrezensionen in seiner Heimat, die von Leuten verfasst würden, die häufig genug noch nicht einmal die Romane, über die sie schrieben und an denen ein Autor vier, fünf oder sechs Jahre verbracht habe, richtig gelesen hätten, um dann zu schließen, er brauche keine Rezensionen: »I have my audience.«[1]

In der Tat, Irving hat weltweit eine riesige Leserschaft gewonnen, alle seine Bücher nach *Garp* sind Bestseller geworden, mittlerweile erscheinen seine Werke in über 30 Sprachen und er hat nach wie vor kein Problem damit, in seinen zahlreichen Interviews genauso wie in seinen Büchern provokant und zugleich ehrlich die Dinge beim Namen zu nennen, egal ob es sich um politische Reizthemen in seiner Heimat handelt, von Abtreibung bis Vietnam, um sexuelle Alltäglichkeiten und Absonderlichkeiten, um den endlos unterstellten, von ihm immer wieder als abwegig bezeichneten autobiographischen Anteil in seinen Erzählungen, den er aber für sein 825-Seiten-Opus *Until I find You* von 2000 akzeptiert, nicht ohne hinzu-

1 Vgl. Joan Smith, »The Salon Interview – John Irving«, 3. März 1997.

zufügen, dass zwischen seinem realen Leben und der Welt seiner Charaktere Welten klaffen. Und in typisch Irving'scher Art schockiert und verzaubert er die Leserinnen der *Brigitte* mit der Überschrift »Ich erzähl euch jetzt was, das wird euch die Hosen ausziehen«,[2] wobei der Ton der Selbstdarstellung wie in all seinen Schriften bei aller Derbheit und ungeschminkter Klarheit der Darstellung nicht verletzt, nicht abrutscht auf sprachliche und inhaltliche Ebenen, die der Wahrheit, einem Leitmotiv seines literarischen Schaffens, der verdichteten Lebenswirklichkeit nicht mehr entsprechen.

Der unvorbelastete Leser des Irving'schen Werks könnte nun auf den Gedanken kommen, es angesichts der skurrilen, vom *mainstream* der Gegenwartsliteratur abweichenden Muster von Geschehnissen zwischen unglaublicher Komik und tief empfundenem Schmerz mit einem ebenso sonderbaren Schöpfer jener Situationen zu tun zu haben, der in seinem Leben alles das praktisch ausgetobt hat, was er in seinem Schreiben abbildet – aber weit gefehlt. Die meisten seiner Leser ahnen nicht, wie konservativ ihr Schriftstelleridol in Wirklichkeit ist, mit elektrischer Schreibmaschine, ohne Notebook, jahrelang in täglicher, harter Arbeit an seinen Büchern feilend, Seite für Seite immer wieder neu schreibend bis das Endergebnis seinem Qualitätsanspruch genügt, in herkömmlicher Familienstruktur und in einem idyllisch abgelegenen Heim in Vermont lebend. So manchem fällt es sicher schwer, sich seinen John Irving so vorzustellen, aber hinter all dem steckt lange, bewusst trainierte Methode.

2 Meike Schnitzler, »Ich erzähl euch was«, in: *Brigitte*, Januar 2006.

Schon als junger Autor formuliert Irving sein Ziel, wie er die Leser erreichen will: durch eine chronologisch geordnete, lineare Erzählweise, die keiner Interpretation durch Rezensenten oder Kritiker bedarf: »I like books that can be read without those middlemen. [...] I hate the elitism, the preciousness, the specialness of so much contemporary fiction. I hate what is turning the novel [...] into something like contemporary painting or contemporary poetry; namely, largely designed for other painters and other poets.«[3]

## John Irvings Weg an die Spitze der Bestsellerlisten – eine biographische Skizze[4]

John Irving wird am 2. März 1942 als John Wallace Blunt, Jr., in Exeter (New Hampshire) als Sohn eines Luftwaffenoffiziers und seiner Frau Helen geboren, die zu den in Neuengland bekannten Winslows gehört, so etwas wie alter Einwandereradel. Die Mutter trennt sich zwei Jahre später vom Vater ihres Sohnes, der seinen leiblichen Vater auch nie kennenlernen wird, aber in seinem Stiefvater, Colin F. N. Irving, einem Lehrer mit dem Spezialgebiet russische Geschichte und Literatur an der Philips Exeter Academy, im Alter von sechs Jahren einen fürsorglichen Vaterersatz und Namensgeber findet; er wird adoptiert und heißt ab 1948 John Winslow Irving. Erst gut fünf-

3 Vgl. Larry McCaffery, »An Interview with John Irving«, in: *Contemporary Literature*, Bd. 23, S. 11.

4 Die kurze Biographie bietet eine Auswahl relevanter Informationen aus Irvings Autobiographie *The Imaginary Girlfriend* (1996) sowie diversen Interviews und Veröffentlichungen über ihn.

zig Jahre später wird John Irving während der Arbeit an *Until I Find You* zufällig von seinem Stiefbruder, zu dem er bis dahin keinen Kontakt hatte, erfahren, wer sein biologischer Vater war, zwei Jahre nach dessen Tod.

John Irving ist eigentlich ein viel zu mittelmäßiger Schüler, als dass er eine Chance gehabt hätte, an der privaten und hochangesehenen Philips Exeter Academy zur Vorbereitung auf das Universitätsstudium angenommen zu werden, da aber sein Vater dort Mitglied des Lehrerkollegiums ist, hat John Anrecht auf einen Studienplatz und schlägt sich mehr schlecht als recht durch, nicht zuletzt weil ihn die damals noch so gut wie unbekannte Lese-Rechtschreib-Schwäche (Dyslexie) in eine ermüdende, als erniedrigend empfundene[5] Sprachtherapie einbindet, die ihn schließlich zu einem Psychiater führt, weil die erwarteten Fortschritte ausbleiben. Aber statt aufzugeben folgt Irving dem Rat seines ersten Trainers im Ringen[6] an seiner Schule, der ihm klar macht, dass es in allem, was man mache, weniger auf Talent als auf eiserne Disziplin und auf Trainingswillen ankomme, und verordnet sich ein beinhartes Rechtschreibtraining mit einer ständig weiter entwickelten Lernliste von ihm falsch geschriebener Wörter; für eine Leseaufgabe, die andere Schüler in einer Stunde bewältigten, setzt er einfach zwei oder drei Stunden an – ohne je darüber zu verzweifeln.

Seine Liebe zum sportlichen Ringen (*wrestling*) be-

5 Vgl. Irving, *The Imaginary Girlfriend*, New York: Ballantine Books, 2002, S. 4 f.

6 Vgl. ebd., S. 8: »[…] it was the first thing I was any good at.«

gleitet Irving bis heute, obwohl er als aktiver Sportler gemäß der Vorhersage seines ersten Trainers nur ins Mittelfeld der nationalen Leistungsklasse vordringt. Dem Umgang mit der Sprache mit dem früh gesteckten Ziel, Schriftsteller zu werden, verschreibt er sich hingegen mit verbissener, erfolgsorientierter Überzeugung, lernt über die an der Schule behandelten kürzeren Werke großer Autoren den Zugang zu deren umfangreichen Romanen, was ihn wiederum durch den Zeitverlust beim Lesen der dicken Wälzer in seinen schulischen Leistungen zurückwirft; aber das alles spielt für ihn keine Rolle mehr, weil sein Vater ihm die Tür zu Tolstoi, Turgenjew und Dostojewski öffnet, sein Lehrer George Bennett ihn zur englischsprachigen und zur Weltliteratur führt, darunter Goethe, Rilke, Musil, Thomas Mann, Böll und Grass, obwohl keiner von all diesen ihn bezüglich der Form des Romans so tiefgreifend beeinflusst wie Charles Dickens, während Graham Greenes Methode (seinem zweiten Vorbild), das letzte Wort des Romans zu schreiben, bevor das erste zu Papier gebracht wird, von Irving als leicht verändertes Prinzip übernommen wird: Er schreibt den letzten Satz seiner Romane, bevor er mit der ersten Seite beginnt – bis heute.

Nach dem Abschluss der Schule beginnt Irving als Neunzehnjähriger ein Englischstudium an der Universität Pittsburgh, erhält ein lächerliches C in seinem Anfängerkurs in produktivem Schreiben, weil sein Kursleiter sich über des Studenten Irving Gebrauch des Semikolons mehr entsetzt als über die Inhalte der Texte, und ist traurig, weil er in Wrestling-Turnieren plötzlich nicht mehr, wie bis dahin im kleinen Exeter üblich, zu den Gewinnern, sondern zu den Verlierern zählt: »But I stopped neither writing nor wrestling as a result of these discouragements.«[7]

Er schreibt sich an der Universität von New Hampshire, Durham, zur Fortsetzung seines Studiums ein, erfährt Zuspruch durch seine dortigen Lehrer (unter anderem die Schriftsteller Tom Williams und John Yount), kann nach einigen Monaten Deutschkurs für ein Jahr (1961/62) in Wien an das Institute for European Studies gehen und lernt Österreich mit seinen historisch bedingten Licht- und Schattenseiten (letzteres vor allem der »Anschluss« während der Nazi-Herrschaft) sowie die Menschen des ›alten Europa‹ bei ausgedehnten Fahrten auf dem Motorrad kennen, heiratet 1964 in Griechenland Shyla Leary, die er kurz vor seiner Abreise nach Wien kennengelernt hat, kehrt noch einmal kurz mit ihr nach Wien zurück, bevor der erste seiner zwei Söhne aus dieser Ehe in den USA geboren wird.

Irving ist nun Familienvater, »married with a child«,[8] und deshalb trotz seiner gerade erst dreiundzwanzig Lebensjahre nach den Rekrutierungsregeln der USA nicht für den Vietnamkrieg verfügbar, schließt sein *undergraduate*-Studium an der University of New Hampshire ab, fasst als verantwortungsbewusster Vater wegen der damit verbundenen Unfallgefahr auch nie mehr sein geliebtes Motorrad an (vgl. den Unfalltod des Protagonisten in *Setting Free the Bears*), setzt sein Graduiertenstudium an der Universität von Iowa fort und schließt es dort (wo Kurt Vonnegut sein Lehrer in *creative writing* ist) mit dem Titel Master of Fine

7 Ebd., S. 68.
8 Ebd., S. 85.

Arts (MFA) ab. Für kurze Zeit verdient er zusammen mit seinem Schriftstellerfreund Don Hendrie mit Saisonarbeit und Gelegenheitsjobs den Unterhalt für seine Familie und schreibt nebenbei an seinem ersten Roman *Setting Free the Bears*, der 1968 erscheint und mit zunächst 7000 verkauften Exemplaren ein erstes ordentliches Einkommen abwirft.

Ein Stipendium der Rockefeller Foundation und diverse Lehraufträge ermöglichen es Irving, das Jahr 1969 wieder in Wien zu verbringen – hier wird auch sein zweiter Sohn geboren. Die Familie hat sich eine Burg als Wohnung gemietet, der Autor arbeitet am Drehbuch zur Verfilmung seines ersten Romans. Insgesamt dauert es nach der Rückkehr in die USA noch bis 1978 – zwei weitere Romane erscheinen, zeitigen aber trotz positiver Rezensionen nur mäßigen wirtschaftlichen Erfolg –, bevor er mit *The World According to Garp* den Durchbruch schafft und an die Spitze der Bestsellerlisten stürmt; nach zwei Jahren sind drei Millionen Exemplare des Buches verkauft,[9] die Zeit wirtschaftlicher Unsicherheit lässt der Sechsunddreißigjährige endgültig hinter sich, während er sein Hobby, das Wrestling, erst 1989 aufgibt, nachdem er jahrelang aus Verbundenheit mit seiner alten Schule neben seinen Söhnen dort noch Schüler trainiert hat.

Es folgen privat einige stürmische Jahre, 1982 die Trennung von seiner ersten Frau, 1987 die Eheschließung mit Janet Turnbull, seiner kanadischen Literaturagentin, im Alter von fünfzig Jahren die Geburt

9 Bis 2005 wurden insgesamt mehr als acht Millionen Exemplare von *Garp* weltweit jeweils zur Hälfte in Englisch und in Übersetzungen verkauft.

seines dritten Sohnes, und in Abständen von durchschnittlich vier Jahren erscheint jeweils ein neuer Irving-Roman auf dem Literaturmarkt.

Längst wird dieser Autor wie ein Star gefeiert, wo immer er auftritt. Als er im Februar 2006 im Rahmen seiner Promotion-Tour für den gerade in deutscher Sprache erschienenen elften Roman *Bis ich dich finde* (*Until I Find You*) in Wien weilt, wo unter dem Motto »Eine Stadt, ein Buch« 100 000 Exemplare seines ersten Romans *Lasst die Bären los* gratis verteilt wurden, feiert ihn das vollbesetzte Burgtheater mit tosendem Beifall. Hier konnte er plötzlich ganz locker über den autobiographischen Anteil in seinem letzten Roman plaudern,[10] was er Jahre zuvor noch zurückgewiesen hätte, und bezüglich der Wertschätzung von Autoren nebenbei fallenlassen, in Europa gebe es mehr Verständnis für Kultur als in seiner Heimat.[11] Mit dreiundsechzig Jahren ist er überzeugt, mehr und härter als je zuvor arbeiten und sich als Schriftsteller noch besser als früher konzentrieren zu können.[12] Die Planungsphase für seinen zwölften Roman, der Ende 2009 unter dem Titel *Last Night in Twisted River* erscheinen soll, hat gerade einmal sechs Monate gedauert.

10 »Man muss lernen, Ausländer zu sein. John Irving im Gespräch«, in: *Kurier*, 19. Februar 2006, S. 23.

11 »Ich bin Ausländer im eigenen Land. John Irving im Burgtheater«, in: *Der Standard*, 21. Februar 2006, S. 28.

12 »Von Kirchenorgeln, Tattoos und Transvestiten. J. Irving zu Gast in Wien«, in: *Wiener Zeitung*, 21. Februar 2006, S. 15.

## Irvings schriftstellerisches Selbstverständnis

John Irving gibt allen angehenden Schriftstellern die Erfahrung mit auf den Weg, dass sie damit rechnen müssen, missverstanden zu werden,[13] und er warnt sie davor, einen Roman als schlecht verhülltes Spiegelbild ihres eigenen Lebens zu konzipieren: »[...] the imagination can select more plausible details than those incredible-but-true details that we remember.«[14]

Einen zweiten Grundsatz beherzigt der Bestsellerautor bis heute: »What I am is a good rewriter; I never get anything right the first time – I just know how to revise and revise.«[15]

Und dann gibt es noch eine dritte Regel, die Irving vom Ringen übernommen hat, die Disziplin, was bedeutet, fast täglich acht Stunden am Schreibtisch zu verbringen, denn wer nach dem Lustprinzip lebe, komme nie auf einen grünen Zweig, also heiße es üben, üben, üben wie beim Ringen und hart arbeiten, bis ein Dialog richtig wirke, eine Figur stimmig sei; das verhalte sich wie die Arbeit eines talentierten Handwerkers, damit am Ende das Buch den Leser unterhält, denn darin sieht Irving die Funktion seiner Romane.

Grundsätzlich betrachtet Irving sich als »old-fashioned novelist«, der sich an den Regeln des Romans des 19. Jahrhunderts orientiert, wie er in einem seiner vielen Interviews ausdrücklich betont: »I believe in plot, in the development of character, in the effect of

13 Vgl. Irving, *The Imaginary Girlfriend*, S. 161.
14 Ebd., S. 157.
15 Ebd., S. 155.

the passage of time […]. And I believe a novel should be as complicated and involved as you're capable of making it.«[16] Das mag auch ein Grund sein, warum Irving kein großer Freund von Kurzgeschichten ist, nur wenige geschrieben hat und sie auch nicht gern liest (»The Pension Grillparzer« ist davon ausgenommen und ihm sehr wichtig). Wenn der Autor seinen berühmten letzten Satz eines neuen Romans erst einmal fixiert hat, beginnt ein langer, zäher, anstrengender Prozess; der Schriftsteller fühlt sich verantwortlich für die detaillierte Entwicklung von Handlungsabläufen und Charakteren, um damit den Leser bei der Stange zu halten und zugleich Respekt und Bewunderung für seine Protagonisten zu erzeugen, indem er sie extremen emotionalen Situationen aussetzt.[17]

Allerdings weiß Irving sehr wohl, dass er mit dieser Art des Erzählens den Bogen manchmal überspannt (»Sometimes I go too far with this«[18]). Immerhin entstehen unter solchen Vorzeichen Romane, die komisch beginnen, gegen Ende aber nachdenklicher und mit jedem Kapitel länger werden, dabei bleibt der Autor wie ein Marionettenspieler Herr seiner Protagonisten. Es bedurfte nach seinen Worten dreier Anfängerromane, bis es ihm gelang, Charaktere zu schaffen, die ihm wirklich etwas bedeuteten, ohne dabei psychoanalytischen, soziologischen oder historischen Trends nachzugeben. »Psychological and sociological interpretations are largely responsible for diminishing literature and for, in many cases, championing the lit-

16 Suzanne Herel, »John Irving«, in: *Mother Jones* (Mai/Juni 1997) S. 2.
17 Vgl. McCaffery, »An Interview«, in: *Contemporary Literature*, S. 12.
18 Ebd., S. 17.

erature that is less imaginative and more plodding […].«[19]

Um den Anspruch zu erfüllen, für seine Leser den optimalen Text abzuliefern, lässt sich Irving auch von Verlegern nicht zur Eile drängen; während ihm das im privaten Alltag nicht gelingt, ist Geduld bei der Arbeit als Schriftsteller eine ungebrochene Maxime,[20] genauso wie das tägliche (!) Schreibpensum, das, wenn dabei mehr als drei oder vier Seiten entstehen, am nächsten Tag eine strikte Überarbeitung fordert, wie überhaupt allein das Schreiben im Mittelpunkt seines Alltags selbst bei langen Reisen steht, nicht mehr das Lesen – damit, so Irving, muss ein Autor abgeschlossen haben, bevor er selbst zu schreiben beginnt.[21]

## Kurzer Einstieg in die phantastisch-reale Welt der Romane John Irvings

Irving wird nicht müde zu betonen, dass nicht eine politische oder sozialkritische Botschaft im Mittelpunkt seines Interesses steht, sondern zwischenmenschliche Beziehungen, er stellt eine Situation, einen Charakter in den Vordergrund seiner Erzählungen, bevor er daran geht, vor dem Hintergrund seines von ihm selbst als altmodisch bezeichneten Wertekanons gesellschaftlich tabuisierte Themen in frappierender Offenheit dem Leser vor Augen zu halten – Gewalttä-

19 Ebd., S. 16.
20 Vgl. Arx (2007), S. 2.
21 Vgl. ebd., S. 5f.

tigkeit, Mord, Terror, Vergewaltigung, Verführung, Abtreibung, echte und entgleiste emanzipatorische Frauenbilder, abstruse Scheinheiligkeit, fragwürdige Mannsbilder: alles das gespiegelt in der sogenannten normalen, bürgerlichen Welt zwischen hoch angesehenen Wissenschaftlern und dem Zwielicht des Rotlichtmilieus, wodurch sich der Sumpf menschlichen Versagens beängstigend vertieft.

Das Thema Sexualität spielt in allen Erzählungen eine wichtige Rolle: »Sex is one of the most important things that happens to people. When you place characters in extreme sexual circumstances, you are able to reveal a lot about them and their natures.«[22] Wo traditionelle Werte sich im Spiel der Geschlechter aufzulösen beginnen, sieht Irving die Gefahr des gesellschaftlichen Verfalls in das Chaos moralischer Leere und setzt dem mit seiner ureigenen Erzählweise, die vielen Lesern vielleicht nie bewusst wird, sein eigenes Lebensprinzip entgegen – »human life will endure.«[23]

Die auf den ersten Blick verstörende Absonderlichkeit vieler Charaktere im Kontext mindestens ebenso ungewöhnlicher Handlungsabläufe hat zahllose Kritiker und Rezensenten immer wieder dazu verleitet, von skurrilen, bizarren, grotesken Erscheinungen zu schreiben; Irving hat das ebenso häufig und manchmal fast aggressiv zurückgewiesen. Vielleicht stimmt aber doch die Aussage, man könne bei seinen Romanen von »grand comedies« sprechen, die äußerste Ex-

22 McCaffery (1982), S. 14.
23 Vgl. Hugh M. Ruppersburg, »John Irving«, in: *Dictionary of Literary Biography*, S. 160.

treme menschlicher Erfahrungen einschlössen: »hatred/love; rebellion/defense; attack/escape, sympathy/persecution.«[24]

Konkret auf seine bis jetzt elf Romane bezogen – und mit einem Seitenblick auf die Erzählung »The Pension Grillparzer« als Teil von *Garp* –, fallen als Schauplätze für entscheidende Geschehnisse gleich zu Anfang und sehr zentral Wien und Österreich ins Auge. Die Hauptstadt der Alpenrepublik, bislang in sieben von Irvings Romanen der Hintergrund, fungiert mit ihrer wechselvollen Geschichte als Zentrale europäischer Machtverwerfungen, mit Glanz und Niedergang, mit ihrer äußeren Schönheit und als Bühne korrupter Menschlichkeit wie eine Metapher für das Leben überhaupt: »Vienna is not merely the setting for lust, disease, and death, however. It is also a place for writing – Jenny, her autobiography; Garp, *The Pension Grillparzer*, a strange but beautiful work of dreams and death.«[25] Doch auch wenn Wien lange Zeit in seinen Büchern der Schauplatz ist, sollten die anderen Handlungsorte in New England, Städte in New Hampshire und Maine, in Kanada, Zentral- und Nordeuropa, Japan und Indien – inzwischen fast weltumspannend – nicht vergessen werden; allerdings stellen die ersten fünf Romane die Regionen Wien/Österreich, Zentraleuropa (Deutschland nur in Randbemerkungen!) sowie New England in den USA in den Mittelpunkt.

24 Vgl. Josie Campbell, *John Irving. A Critical Companion*, Westport (Conn.) 1998, S. 7.
25 Ebd., S. 76.

Besonders augenfällig ist das wiederkehrende Motiv des Zirkus und insbesondere der Bären (sowie einiger weiterer eindrucksvoller Tiere) in Irvings Schriften, und man könnte auf den Gedanken kommen, dass der Zirkus und die darin auftretenden dressierten Tiere den Hintergrund für das niemals endende Schauspiel menschlicher Ängste, Unzulänglichkeiten und Eitelkeiten abgeben (s. Irvings »Notes«, S. 55, zu den Ängsten des Hoteliers angesichts des Bären). Wie der Bär Duna in »The Pension Grillparzer« am Ende der Erzählung an seiner Unfähigkeit zugrunde geht, sich auf die neue Situation, der er ausgesetzt wird, einzustellen, endet der Versuch der Befreiung der Tiere in *Setting Free the Bears* im Chaos; dem Elefantenwärter im Minizirkus von *The Water-Method Man* zertritt sein Dickhäuter drei Finger; der grotesk riesig wirkende Zwerg in *The 158-Pound Marriage* tritt auf wie ein schlecht dressierter, tapsiger Bär neben einer Tänzerin; die Geschichte vom bissigen Hund in *Garp* ist verbunden mit dem Hund als Schlittenzugtier; der sechzigjährige Rechtsanwalt in *The Cider House Rules* lässt sich von einem überdrehten Ehepaar eine Bärengeburt zeigen; der Verkauf des aufgegebenen Hotels an den Zirkus »Fritz« in den USA in *The Hotel New Hampshire* geht weiter mit den Spekulationen der Protagonistenfamilie über das neue Hotel gleichen Namens in Wien mit »whores and bears and spies« und einem jungen Bären namens »Susie the bear«, der sich als liebenswertes junges Mädchen im Bärenfell erweist; die Szenen aus der Tierwelt werden noch skurriler in *A Son of the Circus*, wo der Elefant auf die Schaukel tritt und die Dickhäuter schließlich verärgert ihre Welt in Unordnung bringen oder ein indischer Zirkuslöwe dem unvorsichtigen Reporter die Hand abbeißt, während die Löwinnen aus angemessener Entfernung mit traurigem Verlangen zuschauen.

Obwohl Irving erklärt, Bären seien in seinem Leben gar nicht so wichtig gewesen, gibt er doch zu, dass er während seines Studienaufenthaltes in Wien für einen Zirkusbärbesitzer dessen dressiertes Tier an den Wochenenden versorgt hat und sich bewusst war, dass es sich dabei nicht nur um eine Art großen Hund handelte, sondern um ein durchaus gefährliches Tier, dessen konstant ausdruckslose Augen in einem ebenso ausdruckslos pelzverhangenen Gesicht sich nie veränderten, selbst wenn sich seine Stimmung plötzlich aggressiv gegen seinen Halter wendete.[26] Irving hat die Bedeutung dieser Tiere in seinen Texten immer heruntergespielt, räumt aber ein: »In my fiction I have always felt that as soon as I get the bear on stage, everything is all right. I can focus the reader's attention in specific ways, maybe because most readers are quicker to show sympathy for animals than for other humans.«[27]

Alle diese Informationen über den Autor führen nun zu einigen letzten Erläuterungen rund um »The Pension Grillparzer«.

26 Vgl. Smith (1997), S. 8.
27 McCaffery (1982), S. 7.

## »The Pension Grillparzer« – Kurzgeschichte oder Teil eines Romans?

Wenn man den Autor beim Wort nimmt, wäre »The Pension Grillparzer« ohne *Garp* nicht entstanden, denn während Irving den jungen Garp mitten in der Entstehungsphase des Romans *The World According to Garp* vom Wrestling-Trainer in einen Schriftsteller verwandelte, fühlte er sich genötigt, den Beweis anzutreten, dass Garp ein guter Autor sei.[28] »The Pension Grillparzer«, eines der vielen Beispiele für Geschichten in der Geschichte in den Romanen, hat aber auch seine Berechtigung als eigenständige Kurzgeschichte, wie Irving durch eine Vorabpublikation in der Zeitschrift *Antaeus* (1976, s. Literaturhinweise) klargestellt hat, und erst in Absprache mit dem Lektor des Romans entscheidet er sich für eine Zweiteilung der Short Story im Romanmanuskript.

Der Leser muss selber entscheiden, ob die drei Generationen, die in der Hotelkontrolleursfamilie vereint sind, und alle anderen Figuren in der Pension zu jenen »terminal cases« gehören, deren Schicksal der letzte Satz von *Garp* widerspiegelt,[29] so wie auch die Pension selbst als Arena des Zusammenlebens offensichtlich dem Gesetz der Vergänglichkeit unterworfen ist.

Eigene Erfahrungen haben beim Schreiben der Erzählung unzweifelhaft ihre Rolle gespielt. »Without personal experiences Garp couldn't, or wouldn't have written *The Pension Grillparzer.*«[30] Der junge Irving

28 Vgl. ebd., S. 13f.
29 J. Irving, *Garp*, S. 609 (»[...] we are all terminal cases«).
30 McCaffery (1982), S. 4.

hat als Student die Licht- und Schattenseiten Wiens hinlänglich kennenlernen dürfen, wie zahllose Andeutungen in seinen Büchern verdeutlichen. Man darf sich aber fragen, weshalb er den Schauplatz nach dem lange geschmähten und unterschätzten, erst in der zweiten Hälfte seines Lebens zu Ehren gelangten Dichter und Dramatiker benennt. Warum stellt er die Pension Grillparzer an eine heute noch bestehende Straßenecke, wo es nie eine Herberge dieses Namens gegeben hat, während früher weiter hinten in der Seilergasse eine »Pension Wien« bestand? Warum erfindet er ein »Austrian Tourist Bureau« mit herumreisenden Hotelkontrolleuren, während es beides nie gegeben hat, sondern bis 1972 nur eine »Fremdenverkehrsstelle der Stadt Wien« und ein staatliches Österreichisches Verkehrsbüro? Zwar gab es früher ein Reisebüro namens »Wiener Verkehrsverein«, das für Hotelreservierungen zuständig war,[31] aber wie sollte ein amerikanischer Student ohne internationale Reiseerfahrung in den Sechzigerjahren des letzten Jahrhunderts solche Nuancen im Zentrum des ›alten Kontinents‹ verstehen? Die Kontrolleure (*spies*) eines österreichischen Touristenbüros bleiben in jedem Fall fiktive Figuren des Schriftstellers.

Wer sich allerdings bei der Lektüre von *Garp* fragt,

31 Diese und die folgenden Angaben beruhen auf Auskünften des Vienna Tourist Board / Wien Tourismus. – Das heute noch etwas düster erscheinende Eckhaus Planken-/Seilergasse beherbergt im Erdgeschoss ein Bistro. Ringsherum hat sich eine bunte Mischung der Altstadtgeschäftswelt gehobener Klasse in hell modernisierten Räumen entwickelt – natürlich gibt es dort keine Pensionen oder Hotels, und ein Parken in zweiter Reihe (vgl. die Beschreibung der Ankunft vor der Pension durch den Erzähler, S. 10f.) würde zu völliger Verstopfung der engen Gassen führen.

Der Ort der Handlung, die Ecke Plankengasse/Seilergasse in der Wiener Altstadt

ob das Auftreten der Huren Wiens der Wirklichkeit entspricht, dem sei versichert, dass dieses Gewerbe in der Tat gesetzlich erlaubt (mit amtlichem Ausweis, genannt »Deckel«) florierte; ohne offizielle Bescheinigung sprach man von »Geheimprostituierten«, und diese Situation hat sich bis heute nicht geändert.

So wie Fiktives und Reales sich in diesen kurzen Hinweisen spiegelt, lässt sich auch in den einzelnen Szenen der Erzählung der Wechsel zwischen scheinbar sachlicher Reportage und einem verwirrenden Spiel zwischen Traum und Wirklichkeit verfolgen. Wie es der Großmutter nicht hilft, ihren Traum für sich zu behalten, und sie es der Tochter überlassen muss, ihn weiterzutragen, so verlieren auch alle anderen Figuren ihren Kampf um das Bewahren der ihnen wichtigen Lebensinhalte. Das gilt auch für den Bären, der viel zu lange in eine ihm völlig unnatürliche Rolle gekleidet wird und am Ende jämmerlich zugrunde geht, der Lächerlichkeit preisgegeben, weil er klauenlos (= wehrlos) weder in der Welt des Zirkus noch der des Zoos ein Dasein hat.

Der Wunsch Irvings, seine Geschichte möge für sich sprechen dürfen, soll hier nicht negiert werden, aber eine lockere Sammlung von Aspekten, die weiter zu verfolgen und zu entschlüsseln sich lohnen würde, möge erlaubt sein: die den gesamten Text durchwirkende Symbolkraft von Aussagen und Formulierungen, die Leben und Tod, Werte und Werteverfall, Harmonie und Zerstörung, Vertrauen und Entzweiung, Parallelen von Traum und Realität, Metaphern für Lebenserfahrung widerspiegeln; bizarre Erscheinungen und Situationen und ihre Wirkung auf den Leser; die Kritik an gesellschaftlichen Formen, Vorurteilen (Ungarn, Russen, europäische Hotels[32]); sprachliche Besonderheiten (Ton, Alliteration); autobiographische Verbindungen zwischen der Short Story und dem Autor John Irving – Letzteres ist natürlich nur denen empfohlen, die trotz seiner heftigen Gegenwehr immer weiter deutliche Spiegelungen seines Lebens im Erzählwerk zu entdecken wagen, nicht nur im elften Roman *Until I Find You.*

*Hans-Joachim Lehnig*

32 Zimmer mit Etagenbädern/-toiletten werden auch heute noch ungewöhnlich zahlreich in einfachen Wiener Pensionen und Hotels angeboten, sehr zum Erstaunen vieler Touristen.

# Inhalt